COLLECTING FOR PLEASURE

CHINA

CHINA

BRACKEN BOOKS

Editor Dorothea Hall
Art Editor Gordon Robertson
Production Inger Faulkner

Concept, design and production by
Marshall Cavendish Books
119 Wardour Street
London W1V 3TD

This edition published 1992 by Bracken Books
an imprint of Studio Editions Limited,
Princess House, 50 Eastcastle Street
London W1N 7AP England

© Marshall Cavendish Limited 1990

Typeset by Litho Link Ltd.
Printed and bound in Hong Kong

ISBN 1 85170 912 6

Some of this material was previously published in the Marshall Cavendish partwork *Times Past*

CONTENTS

INTRODUCTION

There is nothing quite like a display of dramatically patterned Art Deco tableware, a group of witty fairings, or a treasured Georgian teapot to bring character and colour to a home. Whatever the reason, collecting antique china has become one of today's most popular pastimes, and the enormously wide range available includes many reasonably priced yet desirable pieces that were once in daily domestic use, ranging from colourful Victorian tea sets, jugs and cow creamers to commemorative ware, Staffordshire ornaments and the humble meat plate.

This well-researched and beautifully illustrated book will help the new collector to acquire the basic know-how necessary to enjoy this satisfying hobby, to avoid the pitfalls and problems associated with collecting, and most importantly, its price guides point out the current market value of china in all its various styles.

Focusing on those periods from which the reader is most likely to find examples, the book identifies the different styles and designs of china. Each piece is clearly photographed and the would-be-collector is told exactly what to look for, how to recognize the work of different designers, craftsmen and women, how to recognize fakes and reproductions, and how to check for damage and repairs.

An invaluable feature of the book is the comprehensive price guide given at the end of each entry: it consists of a

separate panel containing several examples of china of the type and period under discussion, all carefully captioned and price coded. (See the Price Guide below for the key to the price codes.) Most of the pieces of china here illustrated represent the middle to lower section of the market with the addition of one or two rarer pieces for good measure.

By helping the reader to recognize the genuine from the fake, spot real bargains and avoid paying grossly inflated prices, this book makes collecting everyday china an exciting and profitable business as well as a pleasurable pastime that may last forever.

I hope it will encourage you to hunt out 'special' pieces for your collections, give you the self confidence to bid for them at auction and bargain with dealers, where necessary. With the aid of this book you are well on the way to becoming an expert yourself.

Tony Curtis

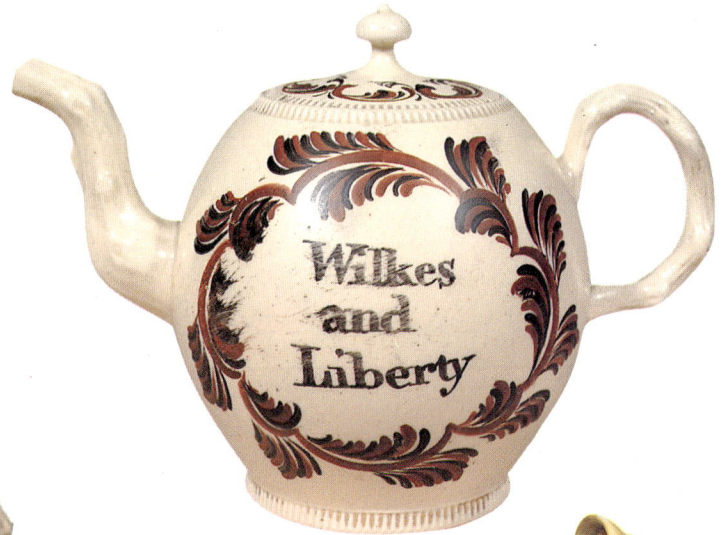

A long pull and a strong pull.

PRICE GUIDE	
KEY	❺ £200-£400
❶ £15-£30	❻ £400-£750
❷ £30-£60	❼ £750-£1500
❸ £60-£100	❽ £1500-£6000
❹ £100-£200	❾ £6,000 plus

Breakfast China

Breakfast in the Victorian country house called for a specialized range of china. Manufacturers responded to the challenge with ingenious and decorative new products

The Victorian breakfast was a far cry from today's quick cup of coffee and half-eaten slice of toast. Even the poor tried to make a meal of it, while for the rich it was a banquet. And to accommodate the many courses, ceramic manufacturers developed a vast new range of colourful breakfast tableware, which can be rediscovered in today's antique shops.

THE ENGLISH BREAKFAST

Before the mid-19th century, breakfast was a highly individual meal, depending on what was available and how one felt. There was no standard breakfast food; people ate what was in their larders from the previous day. Fish and cold meat, as well as bread and cheese, were commonly on the menu. And well into the 18th century these were washed down with ale, or even claret. As tea and coffee became more available, they supplanted alcoholic beverages, with tea the clear favourite.

The French social reformer La Rochefoucauld, exiled to England in 1784, describes the typical breakfast as 'tea and bread and butter of various kinds'. Ten years later Rev. James Woodforde, a Norfolk parson who recorded nearly every meal he ate in his mouth-watering diary, describes a breakfast of 'Chocolate, green and brown Tea, hot Rolls, dried Toast, Bread and Butter, Honey, Tongue, and Ham grated very small'.

Eggs were first introduced to the breakfast table in the 19th century. Mrs Beeton includes them along with dozens of other suitable items in the first edition of *Household Management* in 1861. In describing 'the comfortable meal called breakfast,' in fact, she lists nearly every dish in the house: 'collared and potted meats or fish, cold game or poultry, veal-and-ham pies, game and rumpsteak pies, are all suitable dishes for the table'. For a country house breakfast for 12 she suggests 'rissoles of fish, broiled kidneys, salmi of game, cold grouse, cold beef and ham, savoury omelette, tea, coffee, hot and cold milk; bread, butter, etc', to which she adds the astonishing footnote, 'fried potatoes make a nice little addition.' Twenty years later, in the second edition of *Household Management,* bacon and eggs take pride of place as a standard dish. Apart from the corn flakes, the 20th-

Egg-cup Cruets

THIS STAFFORDSHIRE WILLOW PATTERN EGG-CUP CRUET DATES FROM THE EARLY 19TH CENTURY. A BEAUTIFUL, RARE AND ALMOST PERFECT EXAMPLE SUCH AS THIS IS A VALUABLE PIECE OF CHINA AND, IN FACT, A MUSEUM PIECE. COMPLETE EGG-CUP SETS FROM THE VICTORIA PERIOD ARE HARD TO FIND IN GOOD CONDITION, SO PRICES REFLECT THIS SCARCITY.

century, traditional breakfast had arrived.

Such gargantuan breakfasts would not have been possible without the crockery on which they were served and consumed. It could even be argued that the sumptuous mealtime spreads of wealthy Victorians were the result of a revolution in the manufacture of beautiful and durable china tableware.

CHINA TABLEWARE

Until the 18th century, the manufacture of household china was in a primitive state. Two social developments then coincided to help transform the struggling ceramics industry into one of the great success stories of the 18th and 19th centuries. First of all, people learned to eat with forks, which had only been introduced to Britain in the 17th century. This opened up a new world of eating opportunities to those who did not like getting their fingers greasy. Secondly, the increasing popularity of tea and coffee created a need for pots, cups and saucers

▶ *In a country-style kitchen, breakfast china looks good on an antique pine dresser. At the Victorian breakfast the large decorative platters were used for cold meats such as ham, beef, game pies and tongue which were always served along with hot dishes, as well as toast, muffins and bread and butter.*

◀ *Cream or primrose breakfast china can add a sunny touch to the breakfast room on the most wintery morning. Boiled eggs, toast and muffins formed only one course of the Victorian country-house breakfast. Even in modest homes, grilled fish and kidneys supplemented this simple fare.*

which, as they broke or cracked, continually had to be replaced.

Demand stimulated supply. By the early 19th century, with higher kiln temperatures and new clay mixtures, manufactures were mass-producing inexpensive and attractive china tableware. At the top of the market was bone china – a mixture of china clay, china stone and calcined bones – developed by Spode but also manufactured by Minton, Wedgwood and many others. Stone china and ironstone china, although considerably cheaper, were strong and serviceable everyday ware. Commonly transfer-printed with mock-Chinese patterns in blue on white, they could be found on breakfast tables of town and country houses throughout the land.

BREAKFAST SERVICES

Enterprising manufacturers of tableware created separate ranges, or services, of china for each meal. An 1822 sale of Mason's ironstone china included several breakfast services of various sizes and components. One typical set comprised 'six breakfast cups and saucers, six plates, six egg cups, one muffin plate and cover'. With a capacity of about half a pint, breakfast cups were considerably larger than the standard tea-service cup, while a breakfast

plate was an inch or so wider than a tea plate. A muffin plate was a circular dish with a domed cover for serving hot muffins.

A larger ironstone service of the same date included a different range of extras: six 'cans', one slop bowl, one cream jug, one roll tray, two dishes and two cake plates. 'Cans' were the familiar straight-sided coffee cups, often designed to go with standard tea-cup saucers. Slop bowls were slightly larger than sugar bowls, with which they are frequently confused today. Before refilling a cup with tea, the hostess would empty the dregs into the slop bowl, a custom that has largely died out in the 20th century.

Other pieces of china designed specifically for breakfast included egg-cup stands, often with a tray for spoons, and egg-stands with holes in which boiled eggs could securely rest. Toast racks were sometimes made to accommodate toast spread with jam or butter. More frequently, jams and marmalade were transferred from their jars into decorative pots. Sardine and potted meat pots were similar means of disguising the commercial origin of a product.

At the end of breakfast, faced with this array of magnificent but dirty china, the mistress could leave her place without a thought of washing up. Already the footman would have begun his work.

Table China

The breakfast table at a large Victorian country house was crowded with china.

Directly in front of the mistress, at one end of the table, were the tea and coffee pots. Just behind them, within easy reach, were the milk jugs (both hot and cold), slop basin and sugar basin. Flanking the lady were the cups and saucers – tea to one side, coffee to the other.

Breakfast guests were each provided with small side plates for bread, muffins or toast. Larger plates for cold meat sat on the sideboard. Butter dishes, cruet stands for salt, pepper and mustard, toast racks, jam pots and muffin dishes were spaced along the table.

While silver and glass cruet sets graced the dining table, china and pottery sets were more suitable for the breakfast table. Generally, these were plain and utilitarian although later in the century novelty items in the shape of birds and leaves were popular.

Toast racks were made in varying shapes and sizes. Many larger ones had shallow dishes at either end for marmalade or jam. Egg cups, too, were often incorporated into toast racks. Many were plain, relying on gilding for ornamentation, and others were transfer-printed or lavishly decorated with flowers in relief. The design of jam and honey pots often indicated the container's contents, so that marmalade pots were shaped like oranges and honey pots like beehives. Dishes for potted fish, such as sardines, were also frequently decorated with an ornamental fish.

In the centre of the table were fruit bowls on elegant pedestals and – if there was still room – a vase of flowers.

▲ *Honey pots in the shape of beehives were common pieces of Victorian breakfast china. The thatched lid and legged stand add quaintness to this novelty piece.*

PRICE GUIDE ❸

▲ *Early to mid-19th century honey pot in classic beehive shape. Marmalade containers were often in the shape of an orange.*

PRICE GUIDE ❸

▼ *White china toast rack in a twisted twig-like design. Toast racks were often designed to catch drips from buttered toast.*

PRICE GUIDE ❷

▶ *This fine majolica jam pot in the popular oriental design is elaborately moulded with fans, humming birds and flowers in the ornamental style typical of this English Italianate ware.*

PRICE GUIDE ❺

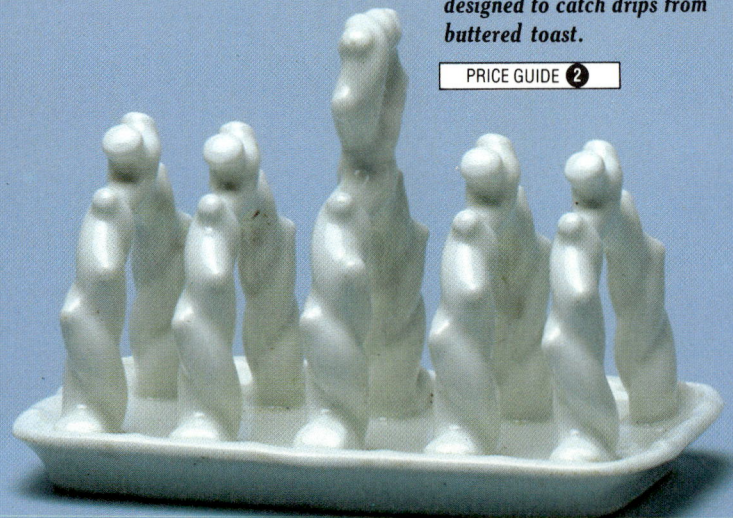

PRICE GUIDE

▲ Late Victorian muffin dish of simple design with a floral border pattern on the rim and plate.

PRICE GUIDE **2**

▲ Muffin dish with leaf decoration in the majolica ware which was so popular in mid-19th century Britain.

PRICE GUIDE **5**

▲ Like many pieces of breakfast china, the contents of this attractive butter pot are indicated by the cow on the lid.

PRICE GUIDE **3**

▲ This novelty butter dish in the shape of a hat is one of the more fanciful examples of Victorian breakfast china.

PRICE GUIDE **5**

▼ This attractive blue-and-white-toast rack is in the imitation delftware that was popular in the second half of the 19th century. True English delft is dated c. 1550-1800.

PRICE GUIDE **4**

▲ Spode Italian blue-and-white ware was a favourite throughout the Victorian era, and this design is still produced today in both dinner and breakfast china.

PRICE GUIDE **4**

▼ A simple but elegant china toast rack in a common Victorian design. Similar smaller racks with only two or three divisions were intended for a one-person's or bachelor's tray.

PRICE GUIDE **3**

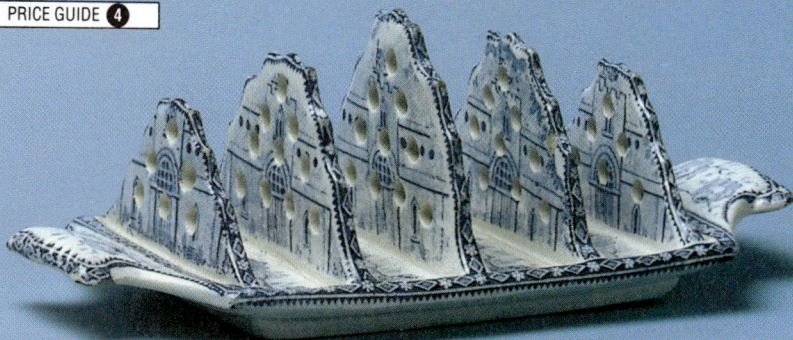

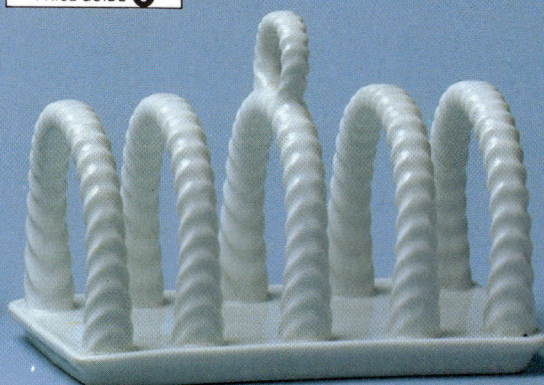

PRICE GUIDE

Serving China

No Victorian breakfast table was large enough for all the food on offer in a country house. To accommodate the overflow, a sideboard was an essential piece of breakfast-room furniture. Covered with its own white cloth, it generally held the cold meats, which supplemented every substantial breakfast. Ham, tongue and chicken or turkey were the least one would expect to find on the sideboard. These were served on the great rectangular or oval platters, often transfer-printed in blue and white. Cold plates for these meats, often with the same design, were also stacked among the platters.

The hot main courses were served from the sideboard. The devilled kidneys, broiled haddock and mutton cutlets appeared on low rectangular serving dishes, while the bacon might arrive in its own covered bacon dish. Attractive chicken tureens kept the boiled eggs warm, and from here they were transferred into egg stands, and then passed onto the table.

What was on the sideboard ultimately depended upon the size of the table and the tastes of the mistress. Frequently the loaf of bread on its platter remained on the sideboard, with slices taken on a bread tray to the table.

▼ *Brightly coloured majolica sardine box with blue-glazed basketware cover and dish. The box top has characteristic relief design with a modelled fish lying on bed of leaves.*

PRICE GUIDE ❹

▲ *These simple, elegant serving platters with a gilded floral design were made for the Goldsmiths' Hall in the 1830s. The muffin dish (right) is late Victorian.*

PRICE GUIDE ❹

◀ *Attractive Staffordshire 'nest eggs', like this example, originated in the mid-19th century and are still produced today for storing eggs.*

PRICE GUIDE ❹

▼ *This fine majolica sardine box, in typical rich colours, contained the salted sardines which were common breakfast fare in Victorian times.*

PRICE GUIDE ❺

▼ *This basket-shaped majolica egg-cup stand with fruit, flower and leaf design is an unusual example of its kind.*

PRICE GUIDE **5**

▲ *These majolica serving platters show the wide range of moulded shapes and designs that could be produced in this stoneware. The brilliant, often strident, colours in greens, oranges and reds are typical of this style.*

PRICE GUIDE **5**

▼ *This egg-cup basket dates from the late 19th century and is notable because it is made of porcelain rather than earthenware.*

PRICE GUIDE **5**

PRICE GUIDE

╡ COLLECTOR'S TIPS ╞

It is very unusual to find a complete Victorian breakfast service in a shop today; if you do, its price will reflect its scarcity. On the other hand, it is relatively easy and inexpensive to start a collection of breakfast odds and ends. You may wish to specialize in one type of item – egg cups or toast racks are particularly attractive to the collector on a budget. Or you may choose to collect only pieces manufactured by one company; or only china in a particular colour or pattern – there is even a club for the enthusiasts of blue and white china. Novelty and souvenir pieces, which were frequently made in breakfast ware, are another area of interest. Jam and honey pots, spanning the Victorian and Edwardian periods, are also worthwhile and fun to collect.

STARTING A COLLECTION

You will not find an antique shop specializing in breakfast china, but most general dealers keep the odd piece from time to time. Larger items such as teapots and serving platters, as well as sets of cups and saucers, are often sold in shops, especially if their age or origin enhance their value. For the smaller pieces – jam pots, cruet sets, egg cups or toast racks, for instance – you will have better luck, and more fun, at antique markets and stalls. Even at sales of bric-a-brac and jumble you can discover breakfast antiques in the most surprising company. Finally, do not be afraid of auctions, where many attractive pieces of china may change hands for well below shop price. Decide what you want before you go, set a spending limit and keep your head. You will probably not be disappointed.

GOOD BUYS

The price of breakfast china, as with all china, depends upon its condition, its age, its manufacturer and its popularity – generally a combination of all the above. Condition is very important. Look carefully for hairline cracks, which can reduce the value of a piece by more than half. Check that the handles of cups, pots and jugs have not been glued on, and look for chips on cups and plates, and around the rim of teapot and coffee pot lids. A Victorian teapot in perfect condition is less common than one would think. (A china coffee pot is a find in itself; most were made of sterling silver and 'old Sheffield' plated silver during the 19th century.) Look also for stains, flaking gilding and worn enamel. Some expert restoration is difficult to detect; if you

Chicken Egg Cups

NOVELTIES SUCH AS THESE HAVE LONG BEEN PRODUCED. THE OPALINE CUP (FAR LEFT) IS LATE VICTORIAN. THE EARTHENWARE CHICKEN (CENTRE) IS EARLY 1800s WHILE THE ONE (LEFT) IS MODERN.

Staffordshire Egg Tureen

STAFFORDSHIRE POTTERS BEGAN PRODUCING THESE EGG CONTAINERS IN THE MIDDLE OF THE 19TH CENTURY. THE NEST, ALMOST ALWAYS IN A YELLOW BASKET PATTERN, FORMED THE BASE WHILE THE HEN SERVED AS THE LID OR COVER. THE NEST EGG (AS IT IS ALSO CALLED) USUALLY RESTED ON THE BREAKFAST SIDEBOARD AND WAS FILLED WITH BOILED EGGS KEPT WARM IN HOT WATER UNTIL EATEN.

CRUDER EARTHENWARE MODELS WERE ALSO KEPT IN THE PANTRY AS A CONTAINER FOR FRESHLY-LAID EGGS.

THIS PARTICULAR EXAMPLE DATES FROM 1860, SO IS AN EARLY – AND WELL-MODELLED – PIECE OF ITS KIND IN A VIGOROUS RANGE OF COLOURS, INCLUDING THE ORANGE, DARK GREEN AND GLOSSY BLACK WHICH WERE POPULAR WITH STAFFORDSHIRE POTTERS AT THIS TIME.

① RELATIVELY WELL-MODELLED BODY, FEATHERS AND TAIL

② VIGOROUS COLOURS, INCLUDING GLASSY BLACK, TYPICAL OF THE PERIOD

③ BASKETWARE BASE WITH THE USUAL BRIGHT YELLOW GLAZE

·CLOSE UP·

① **BUTTER-DISH LID**

② **BASKETWARE IN RELIEF**

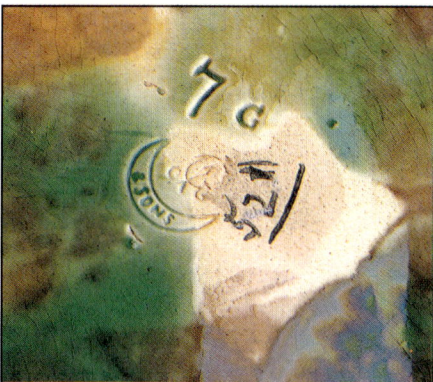

③ **MAKER'S MARK**

④ **MOULDED MAJOLICA**

① CHINA CONTAINER LIDS OFTEN DENOTE THE CONTENTS. COWS APPEAR ON BUTTER DISHES, BEES ON HONEY POTS, ORANGES ON MARMALADE JARS AND FISH ON CHINA SARDINE BOXES.

② BASKET AND CANE WARE WERE ENORMOUSLY POPULAR AS A DECORATIVE STYLE, EITHER ALONE OR AS A BACKGROUND FOR FLORAL OR LEAFY DESIGNS IN RELIEF.

③ THE MAKER'S MARK ON THIS PLATE BELONGS TO GEORGE JONES & SONS, MANUFACTURERS OF MAJOLICA-STYLE WARE FROM 1861, AND WHO CONTINUED TO PRODUCE DECORATIVE EARTHENWARES UNTIL 1951.

④ A WIDE RANGE OF VICTORIAN BREAKFAST AND DINNER WARE WAS PRODUCED IN ENGLISH MAJOLICA STYLE. UNDER GAS LAMPS, THE RICHLY-COLOURED GLAZES GAVE OUT A LUSTROUS GLOW.

⑤ VICTORIAN CHINA TOAST RACKS USUALLY HAD FIVE DIVISIONS, HOLDING FOUR SLICES OF TOAST. MANY HAD WELLS TO COLLECT MELTED BUTTER.

⑥ IMITATION DELFTWARE, MADE FROM THE 1850s BY MINTON AND OTHER POTTERIES, HAS MORE STRIDENT COLOURS THAN EARLY ENGLISH DELFT.

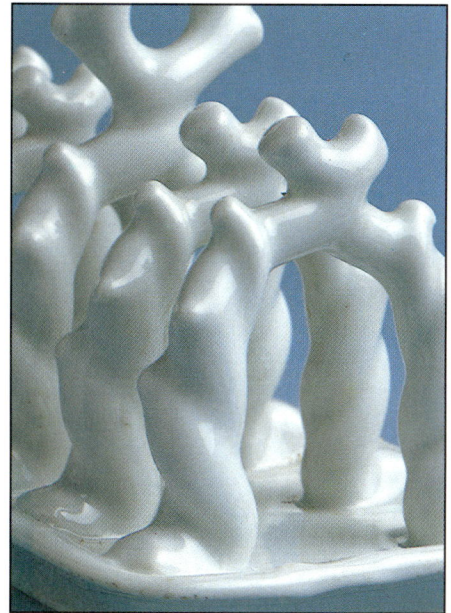

⑤ **TOAST-RACK STYLE**

⑥ **IMITATION DELFTWARE**

are doubtful of its condition or suspect that it has been restored, do not buy an expensive piece of china.

The maker's mark is a sort of price tag on a piece of china. Printed or impressed on the bottoms of individual items, these distinctive designs or initials can sometimes date a piece to the exact year of manufacture. Although there are many attractive pieces of breakfast china that are unmarked, those that have a mark tend to be more valuable. A fine Wedgwood egg cup, for instance, will be more expensive than an unmarked example of the same period and design. A number of books are available to help steer you through the forest of makers'

marks, but unless you are collecting solely for investment, the ultimate value of a piece lies in its value to you.

POINTS TO WATCH

■ Look for hairline cracks in all items of china.

■ Check carefully for signs of repair around vulnerable handles or spouts.

■ Examine gilding for signs of flaking and enamel decorations for wear.

■ Look for chips, especially around edges of cups and plates and inner rims of lids.

■ If buying an expensive piece of china, double-check the maker's mark yourself by referring to a book on the subject.

▲ *This Mason's ironstone china drainer would have been used for fried breakfast foods such as bacon, sausages or fish.*

Dinner Services

The Victorian lady was spoilt for choice when it came to her best china.
From Staffordshire earthenware to Minton bone china, materials were as
varied as the exquisite oriental and pastoral designs

The Victorian dinner service was similar in make-up to the present-day set. It consisted of large and small plates, soup bowls, meat plate, vegetable tureens and comports.

However, the story of the modern English dinner service really begins in the mid-18th century. Although plates, cups and dishes existed before this, geography and industry had conspired to make uniform design a near commercial impossibility.

PORCELAIN AND EARTHENWARE
In 1750, a Doctor Pocock of Bristol discovered a 'soapy rock' which proved to have exceptional resilience and translucence when combined with the 'soft-paste' used in the manufacture of English 'porcelain'. Soft-paste dinner services were made between 1745 and the early 1800s, although a complete set is virtually unknown today.

Doctor Pocock's discovery was taken up by Lund's 'Bristol China Works', which, in turn, was taken over by Doctor John Wall and his Worcester Porcelain Factory, which made real commercial use of it. The inclusion of the 'soapy stone' resulted in a porcelain of exceptionally crisp and elegant design, with a heavier and denser texture.

While developments were happening in porcelain, earthenware and stoneware were maturing along their own lines. Early porcelain was still the preserve of the very wealthy. But the growing middle classes eagerly bought more practical designs.

COMPARISONS
Sèvres Colours

THE BRILLIANT COLOURS OF ORIGINAL SÈVRES WARES INSPIRED 19TH-CENTURY PORCELAIN, PARTICULARLY *BLEU CELESTE* AND *GROS BLEU*.

In 1761, at his Ivy House Works in Burslem, Staffordshire, Josiah Wedgwood introduced a strong, off-white earthenware body, which was combined with a brilliant, cream-coloured glaze that concealed surface blemishes and was impermeable to liquid. This was the first 'creamware'.

In 1776 Wedgwood introduced china clay and china stone into the body, and then reduced the amount of the latter in 1780. This improved version of creamware he called 'pearlware'; he found it ideal for the new fashion of transfer-printing.

MASON'S IRONSTONE

With Wedgwood's decline, from 1810, the brothers George Miles and Charles James Mason came to the forefront. In 1813 they took out a patent for the manufacture of 'ironstone china'. It was made from the glassy molten slag from factories in the area, which was pulverized and added to the clay body. The result was a durable but translucent earthenware.

Quantities of these wares have lasted the century or more until today, including whole and large parts of dinner services, and many separate meat and serving dishes. The patterns were bold, inspired by the Japanese craze of mid-19th century Britain.

SPODE EARTHENWARE

Taking over a Staffordshire factory in 1770, Josiah Spode continued to make inexpensive earthenware tablewares. But he

▼ *Pieces of creamware with leafy border designs form an attractive dinner set.*

▲ *Leaf-shaped earthenware dishes were produced in a range of sizes.*

also began to experiment with transfer-printing on good quality creamware, which proved a great commercial triumph.

Patterns on dinner services varied enormously, but those influenced by oriental motifs predominated; the most popular was the Willow Pattern. The development of multi-coloured transfer-printing in 1830 widened design horizons even further.

By 1805 Spode was also producing stone china, a heavy felspathic earthenware. The preoccupation with felspar continued with the production of felspathic porcelain, which began to appear in the early 1800s and continued to be made into the later Victorian period.

SPODE BONE CHINA

Painted and printed landscapes were also used on bone china, which was the new paste developed by Spode in about 1795. But it was left to his son, Josiah Spode II, and his partner W. T. Copeland, to bring the invention into real prominence. Technically neither a hard-paste nor a soft-paste, bone china was a combination of china clay, china stone and 30-40 per cent bone ash. It was stronger, whiter and more translucent than either of the earlier pastes.

MINTON CHINA

Thomas Minton, who had once worked with Spode, began his own manufacture of bone china a year after its inventor. By the early 1800s his formula was improved and, under his son Herbert, the company of Minton became the most highly regarded in the country. Numerous patterns were used by these and other manufacturers of bone china, including floral bouquets, pastoral scenes and Japanese-inspired arabesques.

Earthenware and Stoneware

The range of wares to tempt a mid-Victorian housewife was enormous. It was the age of experiment, and an enormous variety of 'bodies' were produced by rival manufacturers.

Creamware was first developed by Josiah Wedgwood in the 1760s and continued up to the mid-19th century. A refinement of creamware was pearlware, which was ideal for the new fashion of transfer-printing.

In 1770 Wedgwood developed a fine stoneware called caneware. Up to the mid-1800s this was often used in a bamboo pattern. The faint coloration was usually formed from a blue, green or red enamel underglaze.

Another Wedgwood earthenware was green-glaze. This was named after the lustrous green liquid glaze which covered leaf-shaped dishes, tureens and some sets of dinner ware. By the early 1800s, shades ranged from yellow-green to deep green. Gradually the glaze became thicker and the earthenware more refined.

Mason's Patent Ironstone was most popular between 1813 and 1862. Flowers, birds of paradise and pheasants form the usual central decoration; borders are gilded.

Spode developed his early blue and white patterns on pearlware, but after 1794 he concentrated on bone china. Patterns on table services were extremely varied and included pastoral and Greek-inspired scenes. Chinese motifs were popular, particularly the classic Willow Pattern. This has a pagoda, three-arch bridge, prominent willow tree and three figures, but there are numerous variations. By 1840 practically every home had at least one piece of Willow Pattern ware.

▲ *Green-glazed leaf dish by Wedgwood. The leaf stem forms the handle.* PRICE GUIDE ③

▲ *Lobed pearlware dish dating from 1812. This was an improved version of creamware.* PRICE GUIDE ④

▲ *Ironstone soup plate by Spode.* PRICE GUIDE ③

▶ *Selection of blue, white and gilt soup tureens with lids and underplates.* PRICE GUIDE ④ ⑦

▲ *Mason's Ironstone sauce tureens make attractive showpieces.* PRICE GUIDE ④ ⑤

PRICE GUIDE

▲ The striking design of ironstone china makes it popular as a set or as individual items, such as large and small flat plates and bowls.

PRICE GUIDE ❸

▲ A salad plate by Hamilton overpainted with enamel decoration.

PRICE GUIDE ❺

▲ Purple and blue pie dish decorated with oriental inspired design, c.1830.

PRICE GUIDE ❹

▲ Armorial plate, with coat of arms, personalized inscription and floral border.

PRICE GUIDE ❸

PRICE GUIDE

Porcelain and China

More delicate and costly than earthenware, porcelain has always been the 'best' china in any household. The porcelain makers of the early to mid-1800s continued to experiment with formulas and techniques to produce wares which were visually extravagant and less fragile than earlier examples. The technical breakthrough was bone china, used widely by 1820.

Bone china – the 'English porcelain' – was at the top end of the market. It was produced in almost the whole range of popular Victorian patterns, including Staffordshire blue-and-white, exquisitely detailed landscape sets, and painted and enamelled dinner services.

Felspar porcelain was better quality than bone china. It was developed by Josiah Spode II after 1800. Pure felspar was an exceptionally transluscent ceramic. It was harder than other porcelains and free from surface blemishes. Hand-painted armorial devices and landscapes, oriental scenes and flora and fauna were all featured.

Coalport's felspar was particularly elegant. From the 1820s the factory imitated all the original Sèvres colours, including the legendary turquoise.

Of all the porcelain factories, Worcester wares incorporate most of the fashions in pastes, patterns and shapes which punctuate the story of porcelain. The factory passed through several different hands, including the Flight and Barr families, Chamberlain and, finally, Kerr and Binns.

Worcester bone china and felspar services are highly desirable, especially Chamberlain's apple-green glazes and Japan patterns, the orientally inspired designs of Flight and Barr, and the royal-blue enamelled underglaze, Sèvres-style wares of Kerr and Binns.

▲ Floral pink plate with gilding by Chamberlain's Worcester. These two names were associated from 1783 to 1840.

PRICE GUIDE **4**

▲ Worcester plate showing Carew Castle, signed by J. Stinton. Sets decorated with landscapes were produced by Worcester from 1813.

PRICE GUIDE **5**

PRICE GUIDE

▶ *Porcelain dessert plate by Coalport. A central floral motif was a popular design. The gilded and scalloped edge makes a complementary border.*

PRICE GUIDE **3**

◀ *Comport and plates from a Worcester dessert service, with a painted landscape in the centre and a gilded border. These pieces belong to a set of four comports and 16 dessert plates.*

PRICE GUIDE **8**

▶ *Sèvres-inspired colours such as the turquoise (bleu celeste) on this felspar porcelain plate, were imitated by the Coalport factory in Shropshire from 1813.*

PRICE GUIDE **3**

▼ *Excellent oval Derby plate from the period 1878 to 1890.*

PRICE GUIDE **5**

▼ *Round Derby plate from 1840, which has been slightly rubbed.*

PRICE GUIDE **3**

COLLECTOR'S TIPS

The range of wares open to collectors of 19th century porcelain and pottery is as large as it was for the Victorian housewife. But competition and prices have risen dramatically in the intervening century. Price – and space in the home – dictate that the average collector will acquire only one antique dinner service in a lifetime. The most practical approach is to collect single pieces at a time and thus build up a set at your own convenience.

The best advice for a prospective buyer of a dinner service is to decide on the type of china preferred, pottery or porcelain, and then on the favourite design. Become familiar with the factories that make the chosen set by reading general books on Victorian pottery and porcelain ware. Once familiar with styles, glazes and decorations, examine makers' marks. Scour reputable porcelain shops and small dealers, armed with one of the pocket-sized booklets on makers' marks to ensure an original purchase.

FACTORS AFFECTING VALUE

The size of the service will make a difference to the price. Understandably, most dinner services are no longer complete. But, even so, because Victorian families were large and home-entertaining so popular, it is not unusual to find sets with 18 dinner plates or more, 10 smaller plates, 8 soup bowls and so on. Other, more fragile sets may have lost far more.

The shape of the plates makes a difference to price, as does the number of large pieces surviving: the more tureens, meat dishes and comports, the more expensive will be the service. Even the type of border is important – whether it is pierced, gadrooned with enamel swags or leaves, edged with a simple, one-colour band or heavily gilded. As a general rule, ironstone and china stone are cheaper than creamware, which is less expensive than bone china, which, in turn, is more reasonable than felspar porcelains.

GILDING

Gilding is often a good clue to age and authenticity. Japanned gilding and honey gilding were used on many of the best wares

Earthenware or Porcelain?

THE POPULAR WILLOW PATTERN WAS PRODUCED ON BOTH PORCELAIN AND EARTHENWARE. THE COLOURS ON EARTHENWARE (LEFT) ARE MUCH STRONGER THAN THOSE ON PORCELAIN WHICH APPEAR TRANSLUCENT.

Davenport Porcelain Plate

FOUNDED IN 1793 BY JOHN DAVENPORT, THIS STAFFORDSHIRE FACTORY STARTED BY PRODUCING CREAMWARE AND BLUE-PRINTED EARTHENWARE. PORCELAIN PRODUCTION STARTED AT THE BEGINNING OF THE 19TH CENTURY AND A FACTORY WAS ADDED TO THE WORKS IN 1820.

THE EARLY PORCELAIN WAS OF INFERIOR QUALITY WITH A GREYISH TINGE AND SPARSE DECORATION. PAINTERS WERE EMPLOYED FROM THE DERBY WORKS AND BETTER QUALITY PORCELAIN WAS PRODUCED, IMITATING DERBY DESIGNS. THESE INCLUDED FRUIT AND FLORAL MOTIFS, STILL-LIFES AND LANDSCAPES IN BRILLIANT COLOURS AND GILDING.

(1) COLOURFUL FLORAL DECORATION ON PLAIN WHITE CHINA.

(2) HEAVY GILDING WITH SIGNS OF RUBBING THROUGH AGE.

(3) CURVILINEAR EDGE PICKED UP WITH GILDED LINES.

① GILDED SWAGS

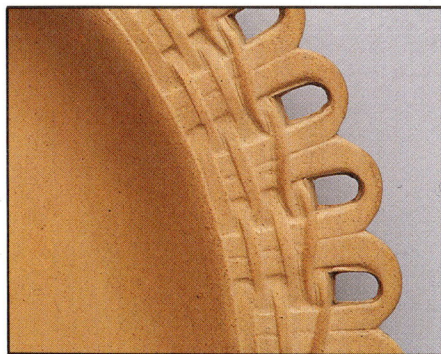

② BASKET-MOULDED CANEWARE

③ FLORAL RESERVE

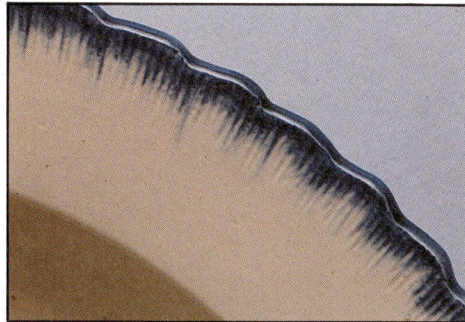

④ BLUE-FEATHERED EDGE

⑤ GADROONED EDGE

① FINISHING PLATES AND BOWLS WITH A GILDED BORDER WAS A POPULAR 19TH-CENTURY TECHNIQUE. MERCURY GILDING IS THE MOST DURABLE AND BRASSY, WHEREAS HONEY GILDING GIVES A MUCH DULLER RESULT.

② TAN-COLOURED CANEWARE WAS PRODUCED BY WEDGWOOD AT THE END OF THE 18TH CENTURY. THE DESIGN OF THIS STONEWARE IMITATED CANE; BAMBOOWARE WAS SIMILAR, IMITATING BAMBOO.

③ THE BLUE DOT BORDER HAS BEEN BROKEN UP AT INTERVALS WITH A FLORAL RESERVE. THE PLATE EDGE AND RAISED PIECES HAVE BEEN PICKED OUT IN GILDING; THESE AREAS ARE VULNERABLE TO RUBBING.

④ FEATHERING THE EDGE OF PLATES WAS A COMMON DEVICE OF THE 19TH CENTURY, USED BY MANY DIFFERENT FACTORIES. THE EDGE OF THIS PEARLWARE PLATE HAS BEEN DELICATELY SCALLOPED AND FEATHERED IN BLUE.

⑤ A GADROONED EDGE IS A SUCCESSION OF CURVES. THIS SOUP PLATE IS DECORATED WITH THE JAPANESE IMARI PATTERN, NOTABLE FOR ITS RICH COLOURS.

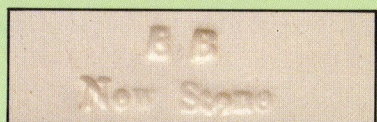

MAKER'S MARKS

TOP: THE ROYAL ARMS WITH SIMPLE QUARTERED SHIELD APPEAR ON CHINA AFTER 1837.
CENTRE: DAVENPORT MARK FROM 1870 TO 1886.
BOTTOM: BB STANDS FOR 'BEST BODY' ON MID-19TH CENTURY CHINA.

until the 1850s, producing a subtle, burnished gold. However, honey gilding was never used on bone china. For this, solid gilding was introduced in 1810, which gave the china a glittering effect; on lesser pieces it may look cheap and hard. Handles and raised decoration were often deliberately left dull as they were subject to rubbing.

Although mercury gilding was invented in the 1780s, it was not in common use until the 1830s, when it appeared on all types of wares. It was exceptionally resilient and permanent, but appeared brassier than other forms of gilding – especially true now, after the passage of time. Transfer-gilding became usual in the 1850s and liquid gold appeared in the 1860s. Both of these have an exceedingly brilliant finish.

POINTS TO WATCH

■ Until 1828, detail painting for landscapes was enamelled over the glaze. Thereafter underglaze printing was common as colours and techniques became available.
■ The standard Japan ware declined after 1830, when chemical paints became common. Colours were harsher and less carefully applied.
■ If a piece is crazed, the irregular criss-crossing lines should be fairly close together. In fakes the crazing is widely spaced.
■ Sèvres-inspired pieces, particularly by Coalport and Worcester, can be distinguished from original French examples by the paste, enamel colours and glaze. The gilding is also much thinner.

A warming plate from the Spode factory with an armorial motif in the centre. Hot water was poured into the lip or spout and plates placed on top to warm.

The Meat Plate

Lavish meals with numerous courses were the order of the day during Victorian times. A whole gamut of specialized servicing dishes were required, including the impressive meat plate

Among the numerous dishes and platters which were part of the Victorian dinner service, there was always at least one pair of meat plates, often more. These were the very largest items and were designed for serving the enormous joints consumed at family and formal dinners. Entertaining was an important part of Victorian life but a family meal was just as serious a ritual. In those days, families were generally large and in middle-class homes it was quite usual to have three or four vast services to cope with a variety of occasions and the enormous meals that were served.

Meat plates were generally rectangular, although an oval shape was not uncommon. Some of the larger ones were particularly functional in design, with a deep well at one end which was served by a leaf-shaped arrangement of sunken channels. In this way the meat juices would collect ready to be ladled over the joint. Because of this design, which originated in the heavy pewter dishes of the 17th and 18th centuries, the plates had to be thickly potted. On the underside of most of these plates, a curved stand was moulded at the opposite end to the well. Others were fixed into separate iron stands with large handles incorporated which made the plates easier to carry.

Victorian dinner services were made of either earthenware, or bone china. Bone china was largely the preserve of the wealthier classes while earthenware was used by the majority of people, even the rich on less formal occasions. The quality and cost of earthenware services was governed by the clay and type of decoration used.

IRONSTONE
One type that was developed became extremely popular. This was 'ironstone', a particularly tough and durable ceramic which resembled fine stoneware. The original patent was brought out in the early 19th century by Charles James Mason, partnered by his brother, George. Once the patent had run out in 1827, the great success of the Mason's ironstone prompted many rival potteries to make their own versions of ironstone.

Of the bewildering choice of patterns available to the Victorian householder, oriental-style motifs, including Japan patterns, were very widely used. The vast majority of mass-produced pottery was decorated with transfer prints, usually blue on white – for instance, the famous Willow pattern – although other colours such as pink, green and brown on white were also used.

By the middle of the Victorian period, hand-painting was virtually confined to very expensive services. Sometimes transfer prints were overpainted but this particular method was usually confined to the lesser quality services.

As well as the popular oriental-style designs, there were romantic scenes of town and country. Hunting and animal themes were also popular as well as the innumerable floral designs. Some of the better quality services were given added interest by depicting different scenes on each size of plate or serving dish.

GUESTS FOR DINNER
At a formal meal when guests were present, the number of serving dishes required was vast. A typical menu might quite often include four separate courses even before dessert. Within each of these courses there was often a choice of four dishes requiring, in all, several meat plates for serving.

▲ The thriving pottery industry centred in and around Staffordshire turned out an enormous amount of everyday dinner wares during the Victorian period. Many substantial meat platters have survived to the present day, no doubt because the larger plates were very thickly potted for extra strength and designed for constant use.

▼ *Formal dinner parties provided an opportunity to dress the table with a fabulous array of the best silver, glass and table ornaments. The finest dinner services were made of bone china and pieces could number well over a hundred.*

The first course usually consisted of two soups and two different types of fish, the latter elegantly presented at the table on plates similar to the meat dishes, only smaller. The entrées were meat, perhaps veal or mutton cutlets, or, as alternatives, lobster patties or boiled marrow on toast, over which melted butter was poured.

After the entrées were cleared, the next course was placed on the table. This was often roast beef, saddle of mutton or braised goose, together with boiled fowls and bacon cheek, all of which required the use of large meat dishes. The third course included one or two further savouries, usually game (when in season) such as wild duck or partridge, followed by up to six puddings.

Roasting, baking, braising, grilling and frying were all frequently-used methods of cooking meat. Roasting was a particular favourite because it gave the joint a delicious aromatic flavour. In the last century, 'roasting' meant spit-roasting before a hot fire, not baking in an oven. This was only possible in homes whose kitchens were fitted with an 'open' as opposed to a 'closed' range.

About half an hour before cooking was due to start, the front of the fire grate was built up with small lumps of coal, while the back was filled with larger, slightly dampened pieces. The small pieces burnt away rapidly but the slower burning embers behind would be bright and hot. These were then brought forward and a metal meat screen, called a 'hastener', placed in front to reflect the heat from the fire. The joint was turned mechanically with a spit jack or 'bottle jack', a patent wind-up mechanical gadget. It was quickly sealed by the even heat thrown out from the screen, then after 10 to 15 minutes, it was moved further away and roasted slowly until nicely browned. Finally, a little salt was sprinkled over the meat just before serving.

CARVING AND SERVING

The way in which meals themselves were served varied depending on the household. In some houses, the butler was called upon to carve and distribute the

Decorative Platters

◀◀ LANDSCAPES AND VIEWS ADAPTED FROM DRAWINGS AND ENGRAVINGS, TOGETHER WITH BROAD FLORAL OR ITALIANATE SCROLLED BORDERS, WERE A COMMON FORM OF DECORATION ON VICTORIAN PLATES. CERTAIN DINNER SERVICES EVEN DEPICTED A DIFFERENT SCENE ON INDIVIDUAL LARGE MEAT PLATTERS.

▶▶ TRANSFER-PRINTED DESIGNS ACCOUNTED FOR A GREAT PROPORTION OF 19TH CENTURY TABLE WARES. THESE WERE CHARACTERIZED BY SINGLE COLOUR PATTERNS ON WHITE, SUCH AS BLUE, PINK, GREEN OR BROWN. INTRICATE AND VERY VARIED DESIGNS WERE PRODUCED THROUGH SEVERAL STAGES, THE FIRST BEING ENGRAVING.

food from the sideboard. But dishes could just as well be placed directly onto the table, in which case the master himself would perform the task of carving while the butler or footman assisted with serving.

Serving began with the first person, almost invariably a female, seated to the right of the host. It was a friendly custom for strangers to be placed here too, when invited to a large family gathering. The order of serving proceeded down one side of the table, then up the other side. If two separate dishes were being served, these would be passed from the top and bottom of the table.

Not only did the host carve the meat but also the fish, when this was offered as well as soup at the first course. The meat dishes holding the most important items of the second course – for instance, the roast beef and the braised goose – were set before the host and hostess, while the minor dishes – the boiled fowls and bacon cheek or their equivalent – were placed on opposite sides of the centre of the table. All were brought to the host when required.

Plates were removed as soon as they were emptied, with those of the host and hostess removed last as a matter of etiquette. As each course was finished, crockery and cutlery were cleared away and fresh knives and forks laid on the table. Meanwhile, the kitchen staff brought up the next course and put it on the sideboard ready to be transferred to the table.

·PRICE GUIDE·⟩ **PLATES AND UTENSILS**

Individual meat plates dating from the 19th century can be surprisingly valuable today, many costing well over £100 to buy. Look out for complete sets and hallmarked silver-mounted utensils for investment value.

◀ *This fine example of a blue and white transfer-print meat plate, with well to collect juices, dates from the late 19th century.*

PRICE GUIDE ⑤

▼ *The sauce tureen, like this one standing on its own matching plate, has disappeared from today's dinner services.*

PRICE GUIDE ④

▼ *Knife rests for carving implements were essential for protecting the table linen. Horn-mounted with silver, solid silver or plate are examples commonly found, and in very varied styles.*

PRICE GUIDE ⑤

▲ *A large platter for serving turkey was indispensable on Christmas Day. These decorative plates can still be put to good use, if only on special occasions.*

◀ *Typically Victorian in shape and design, this sauce tureen displays heavy, scroll handles and acorn-lid top.*

PRICE GUIDE ④

Buying Meat

THE LARGE AMOUNT OF MEAT CONSUMED BY THE VICTORIANS CAME FROM A VARIETY OF SOURCES. IN LARGER ESTABLISHMENTS, MANY OF THE PROVISIONS WERE DELIVERED ON A DAILY BASIS BY THE VARIOUS TRADESMEN WITH WHOM IT WAS THE COOK'S DUTY TO DO BUSINESS. YET BETTER QUALITY WOULD INVARIABLY BE OBTAINED BY GOING OUT AND SELECTING THE CHOICEST PIECES ONESELF. ONCE BOUGHT, THE MEAT HAD TO BE HUNG FOR A FEW DAYS IN THE LARDER TO TENDERIZE IT, THEN, TO PREVENT IT FROM GOING BAD, IT WAS OFTEN SALTED. SMALL SHOPS WERE SUPPLIED VIA THE LARGE MEAT MARKETS, OF WHICH SMITHFIELDS IN LONDON (RIGHT) WAS THE MOST FAMOUS. DURING THE SHOOTING SEASON, THE LARDER WOULD BE SUPPLEMENTED WITH GAME BROUGHT HOME BY THE GENTLEMAN OF THE HOUSE.

The carving implements used by the Victorians were as sharp and efficient as any in use today. The knives and forks were of the finest Sheffield steel, often with staghorn handles mounted with silver. The knives, forks and matching sharpeners, or steels, were frequently sold in velvet-lined presentation cases. When used at the table, the knife blade was placed on a special knife rest of cut glass, silver or silver plate in order to protect the linen.

When each course was completed the serving dishes, crockery and cutlery were cleared onto the sideboard. As the next course was brought upstairs from the kitchen and handed to the servant waiting at the table, the kitchen staff would take down the remains of the previous course. Leftovers were frequently turned into soup or patties.

When the savoury courses and puddings were finally over, the whole table was cleared, and a fresh cloth laid with a special service for dessert, a course consisting simply of fruit and ices to finish the meal.

▼ *Ceramic sauce ladles bearing blue and white designs. Chinese-inspired motifs were among the most popular patterns on table ware.*

PRICE GUIDE ❸

▲ *The Victorians were very fond of nature-inspired patterns on their dinner ware. This standard platter has a neat border of pink primulas and leaves.*

PRICE GUIDE ❹

▶ *The Davenport pottery was renowned for its fine quality earthenware and stoneware. This ridged meat plate with holly design is dated c.1850.*

PRICE GUIDE ❺

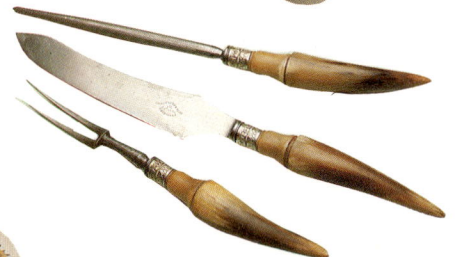

▲ *Matching carving knives, forks and sharpening steels were frequently embellished with embossed silver mountings. These have ivory and staghorn handles.*

PRICE GUIDE ❺

Tea Sets

Taking afternoon tea in the conservatory or parlour was a high point in the Victorian domestic routine, and the most delicate and decorative china was reserved for serving this refreshing beverage

The Victorians transformed the ancient custom of tea drinking into a British institution, and every household practised the daily ritual of serving tea in the afternoon. The Eastern blends, taken black or in the British manner with a little milk and sugar, were served in finely modelled tea sets – their ornate shapes and patterns reflecting the elaborate Victorian style.

No afternoon was complete without the serving of tea and cakes. The early dusks of winter in the drawing room were brightened with the arrival of the maid with her tray, while in warm summers the bright, airy conservatory with its profusion of exotic plants made an excellent setting in which to drink the refreshing China and Indian teas, served from fine, floral-decorated china.

THE CHINESE SERVICE

When tea drinking became a fashionable pastime in Europe in the 17th century, tea was a luxury item imported from the East. Not unnaturally, all the necessary equipment – tea bowls, saucers and teapots

▶ *With the introduction of bone china, tea sets became more widely available than ever before. New methods of manufacture and decoration led to mass production, and sets such as this attractive transfer-printed and hand-painted cabaret set were made in vast numbers.*

– was imported in the same period. Great numbers of these early 'tea sets' accompanied the vast shipments of tea – not only was demand for the attractive wares high, but practicality dictated that the lowest (and wettest) levels of the ships be filled with non-perishable produce. It was therefore profitable for shipping merchants to stock the holds with crates of the popular blue and white china which can still be found today.

These Chinese wares, made from fine porcelain, were imitated by continental manufacturers, who produced their own porcelain sets based almost entirely on oriental designs. Throughout much of the 18th century, tea was supped from Chinese-style bowls and it was not until the 1770s

◀ *This richly decorated Japan-patterned cabaret set, made around 1860 by Ashworth, reflects the Victorians' continuing love of exotic oriental designs.*

Around much the same time, developments were taking place in the Mason Brothers factory which resulted in 'Patent Ironstone China', made from a finely powdered felspathic rock or stone added to a stoneware or clay body. The new material, favoured for its cheapness and durability, was quickly adopted by other manufacturers, who used names like 'Stone China' or 'Opaque Porcelain'. Although manufacturers used the words 'china' and 'porcelain', the ironstone was more like a very dense and strong stoneware.

SHAPE AND STYLE

Tea service styles were developing and changing constantly according to fashion. Early 19th century services were produced with 12 cups and saucers, the components resembling the sets of today. A Spode invoice of 1810 lists a set consisting of: a teapot with stand; a sugar box; a milk ewer; a slop bowl; two bread plates; 12 tea cups; 12 coffee cans (cups); 12 saucers. Only one set of 12 saucers was provided for both the tea cups and coffee cups on the assumption that the two would never be used simultaneously. Individual plates were missing from sets of this period, as prior to the 1840s, toasts, scones and muffins were eaten in fingers straight from the bread plates, or off toasting forks. The Victorians considered this ungenteel, and because china had become so much cheaper, extra plates and saucers were added to the sets.

By the middle of the 19th century, the tea cup had developed a recognizable shape. The bowl of the cup was shallow and wide, and it often had a handle of complex shape. Decoration varied according to the material used. Creamware and some fine stonewares were hand-painted, as was bone china. Other wares were decorated with both hand-painting and transfer-printed patterns.

VARIATIONS ON A THEME

In wealthier households, silver teapots, sugar bowls and cream jugs were often used in preference to china, so these items were frequently supplied as optional parts of the set. Antique sets found today which lack these pieces may not, therefore, be incomplete, but merely intended for use with the rather grander silver or plate three-piece teapot sets.

Variations on the large (and expensive) theme of 12 were also popular. Cabaret sets were widely available – these usually consisted of one or two cups and saucers, a tea pot, sugar bowl, slop bowl and cream jug, all on a matching tray.

that cups with handles began to appear.

The 19th century saw further developments both in style and materials. Manufacturers constantly experimented with new methods of production, concentrating particularly on hard paste porcelain, which was a very expensive commodity. Few materials had such brilliance and translucency when fired, but cost and kiln losses were high.

BONE CHINA AND IRONSTONE

The result of these extensive trials was the development of bone china. It was discovered by Josiah Spode that the addition of bone ash, china clay and china stone, to the refined clay body produced a white china of good translucency at a reasonable cost. Bone china largely replaced porcelain, except for the very finest services.

Fine Bone China

Bone-china tea sets are most typical of the Victorian period. The delicate, translucent material was developed and made in Britain, and enormous quantities were exported to the continent. The better quality sets were hand-painted, often with floral motifs, and enriched with gilding of excellent quality.

Cups from the mid-Victorian period had much of the decoration inside the bowl – decoration on the outside was restricted to simple gilded lining or motifs – as the inner rim was more visible than the outside with the shallow tea cup shapes. Coffee cups were generally taller and straighter than tea cups, although when seen alone it is sometimes hard to tell the difference between them.

Most of the 19th century manufacturers impressed or stamped their wares with an identifiable mark. Occasionally pieces can be found marked with the name of a shop or store – this indicates that the shop bought an exclusive line.

▶ *Blue, cream and rose-patterned Staffordshire tea cup, coffee cup and saucer, c. 1845. The insides of the cups are highly decorated with a blue band and rose design, with gilt leaves.*

| PRICE GUIDE ❹ |

▼ *Staffordshire coffee cup and saucer decorated with hand-painted gilt flowers and green foliage, c. 1840. The decorative handle is also painted with a floral design.*

| PRICE GUIDE ❸ |

| PRICE GUIDE |

◀ *Late Victorian pink and white bone-china tea cups and saucers with matching plates and milk jug. The delicate leaf-mould design is set off with hand-painted gilding on the rims, cup bases and handles. The handle design is known as the crabstock pattern.*

PRICE GUIDE ④

▼ *Derby bone-china teapot with matching cup and saucer, c. 1825. The banded gilt and black scrolled pattern is repeated on each piece, and the teapot has additional gilding on the handle, spout and lid. Ornately designed tea pots were very popular in the early 19th century.*

PRICE GUIDE ⑤

◀ *Staffordshire bone-china tea cup and coffee cup with saucer, c. 1835, decorated with a rich blue band on the inner rims of the cup and saucer, and finished with hand-painted gilding in floral designs.*

PRICE GUIDE ③

▼ *A mid-Victorian cream and pink bone-china tea cup and saucer, transfer-printed with an attractive floral design. Hand-painted gilding has been added to the cup rim, base and handle and to the saucer rim.*

PRICE GUIDE ③

PRICE GUIDE

Japan-Patterned Stone China

Japanese patterns have been subject to cycles of popularity since porcelain was first made in Europe. The continental factories took their inspiration from the Japanese paintings of trees and flowers and fine brocaded silks, and such was the appeal of these wares that the potteries began experimenting with oriental designs with the aim of producing them for a less exclusive market. At the end of the 18th century, the Staffordshire manufacturers mastered the necessary techniques and beautiful Japan-patterned china became available to all classes for the first time.

One of the enduringly famous makers linked with the style was Masons – the originator of ironstone china, the stoneware body from which all other stone chinas are derived. Most commonly found is the Kakeimon style, which can be distinguished by the asymmetrical forms, particularly of trees and flowers. The European imitators tended to follow fairly closely the palette of the Japanese originals, in which a distinctive deep blue and a brilliant red are most prominent.

Imari patterns were popular for all types of china. These strongly coloured designs are broken into segments by bands of ground colour with the reserves decorated with stylized flowers and gilding.

After 1825, Japan patterns were mass produced, many of the wares coming from unnamed Staffordshire potteries. These were characterized by poorer quality colour and form.

▶ A late Victorian, Japan-patterned tea pot. The painted gilding has been used to striking effect on the spout, handle, rim and body.

PRICE GUIDE 3

▼ *Minton stoneware tea cup and saucer with attractive, Japan-patterned floral design on a white background, c. 1840. Both the cup and saucer are stamped with the mark* 'AMHERST' *Japan.*

PRICE GUIDE ❸

▲ *Japan-patterned tea cup and coffee cup with matching saucers, both from Derby. The tea cup is c. 1830, the coffee cup c. 1900. The deep blue sections decorated with red flowers and green foliage are repeated around the inside rim of the cups. Similar patterns are still produced today.*

PRICE GUIDE ❹

▶ *Staffordshire coffee cup and saucer c. 1880 depicting grasses painted on a white background. The design shows an oriental influence. The small, round handle on the cup has been painted to resemble bamboo, matching the inner rim on the saucer.*

PRICE GUIDE ❷

PRICE GUIDE

Victorian tea sets were made for 12 people, and it is not too difficult to obtain a set which, while technically incomplete, still has sufficient pieces for six. It is possible to find good sets of bone china, particularly in country areas, for under £100, although really fine examples by important makers, or a well-decorated porcelain set, would command a much higher price. An attractive service can make a good focal point in a cabinet as well as being functional. It is worth remembering that although bone china looks extremely fragile, it is no more so than good modern tea ware.

While a complete set often commands a price in excess of the sum of its components, individual cups and saucers can form an attractive collection. Unless a piece is interesting from a technical point of view – perhaps a particularly early or rare example of a process – it is seldom worth acquiring pieces that have suffered damage.

CRACKS AND DAMAGE

Hairline cracks, at first almost invisible, become discoloured and obvious after a time. While it is sometimes possible to remove some of the staining with bleach, it is not always effective and can give rise to additional, though different, staining.

CARE AND RESTORATION

One of the joys of china collecting is that, beyond normal careful handling, there is little else to guard against. Damp, sunlight and woodworm – the enemies of most types of antiques – have no damaging effect on china. It is not advisable, however, to put delicate ceramics in a dishwasher. Good tea sets should always be washed by hand.

Porcelain and other ceramic restoration is expensive when undertaken professionally

Enduring Designs

MANY JAPAN PATTERNS WERE SO SUCCESSFUL THAT THEY WERE PRODUCED IN EXACTLY THE SAME FORM FOR DECADES. THE TEA CUP ON THE LEFT WAS PRODUCED AROUND 1830, WHILE THE COFFEE CUP ON THE RIGHT IS DATED 1900.

Delicate Bone China

THE VICTORIANS WERE ESPECIALLY FOND OF SMALL AND DELICATE BONE CHINA TEA SETS, AND, AS THEY WERE SO MUCH CHEAPER THAN IMPORTED PORCELAIN, THEY WERE ABLE TO USE THEM REGULARLY.

THIS PARTICULARLY ATTRACTIVE PINK AND WHITE LEAF-MOULD DESIGN IS UNMARKED, BUT WAS A COMMON STYLE PRODUCED BY MANY FACTORIES IN THE LATE VICTORIAN PERIOD.

'MARRIAGES' WITH THIS TYPE OF SET ARE COMMON, SO ALWAYS CHECK THE CUP AND SAUCER INDIVIDUALLY FOR ANY DIFFERENCES IN PATTERN AND TONE.

HAIR CRACKS ARE OFTEN ONLY SEEN WITH THE MAGNIFYING GLASS – HOLD EACH PIECE UP TO THE LIGHT AND EXAMINE CAREFULLY.

HANDLES ON THIS PARTICULAR TYPE OF SET ARE SUSCEPTIBLE TO BREAKAGES. MAKE SURE THE HANDLE HAS NOT BEEN REPAIRED AND CAREFULLY RE-GILDED.

① LEAF-MOULD PATTERN COMMONLY PRODUCED IN THE LATE 19TH CENTURY

② TWO-TONE COLOUR EFFECT

③ CRABSTOCK HANDLE DESIGN

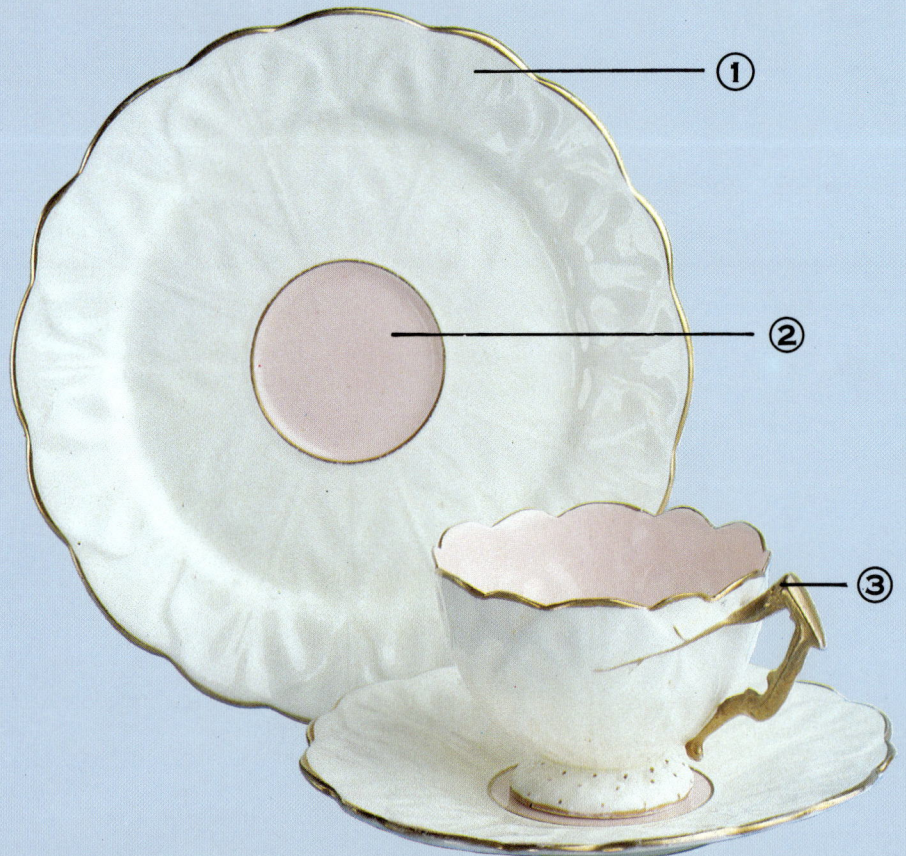

① TRANSFER-PRINTING

② HAND-PAINTING

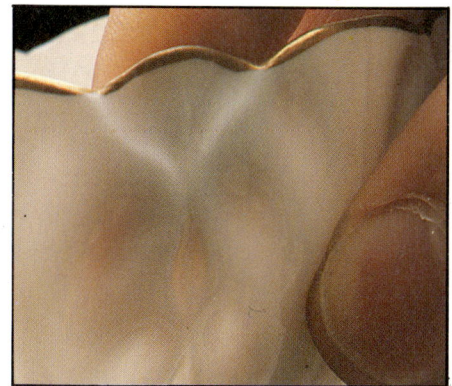
③ TRANSLUCENT FINE BONE CHINA

① TRANSFER-PRINTING IS A METHOD, FIRST DISCOVERED IN THE 1750S, OF PRINTING A PATTERN OR DESIGN ONTO CERAMICS. THE DESIGN WAS INITIALLY ENGRAVED ONTO A COPPER PLATE, RUBBED WITH PIGMENT MIXED WITH OILS, AND THEN TRANSFERRED TO A SHEET OF TISSUE PAPER WHICH WAS PRESSED ONTO THE OBJECT. BOTH WERE THEN IMMERSED IN WATER. OCCASIONAL OVERLAPS OR MISMATCHING OF THE PATTERN OCCUR WHICH MAKE TRANSFER-PRINTING EASY TO IDENTIFY.

② 19TH CENTURY CHINA WAS LARGELY HAND PAINTED AND MUCH IS FINELY EXECUTED.

③ FINE BONE CHINA WAS FAMED FOR ITS TRANSLUCENCY — HOLD A CUP TO THE LIGHT WITH A FINGER BEHIND TO CHECK THE QUALITY.

④ THIS SIMPLE CURVED CUP HANDLE IS SLIGHTLY ELONGATED — IT WAS HELD BETWEEN THUMB AND TWO FINGERS.

⑤ THIS DISTINCTIVE ANGULAR HANDLE WAS MORE DECORATIVE THAN PRACTICAL.

⑥ HANDLE PAINTED TO RESEMBLE BAMBOO, AND HELD WITH THUMB AND FINGERS.

④ ELONGATED HANDLE

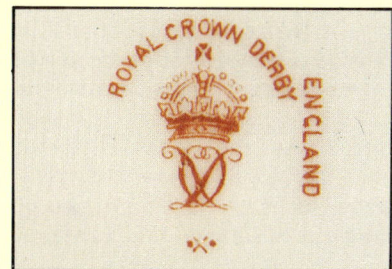
⑤ ANGULAR HANDLE

⑥ 'BAMBOO' HANDLE

MAKERS' MARKS
MOST 19TH CENTURY CHINA CARRIED A MARK OR STAMP IDENTIFYING THE MANUFACTURER. THESE CAN HELP DATE PIECES. THE AMHERST JAPAN, FOR EXAMPLE, IS C. 1840, THE CROWN DERBY C. 1900.

and seldom worthwhile in terms of cost, unless a piece is particularly fine. Home restoration is an interesting and absorbing hobby, but care and patience are needed for good results. Be sure to read up on the subject extensively before tackling anything yourself (there is a wide range of books on ceramic restoration available).

CHOICE AND AVAILABILITY
In terms of choice, purchasers can find examples of most kinds of tea wares to suit their own tastes and pockets. Many general antique shops and most antique markets will have both complete sets and individual pieces. The major auction houses conduct specialist sales at which complete tea sets often appear, and it is worth scouring the antique fairs for ceramic stalls who specialize in tea and coffee wares.

POINTS TO WATCH
■ Always ensure that all pieces are perfect — handles that have been re-attached are easily broken again.
■ Check for hair cracks in bone china by holding the object up to the light with a magnifying glass.
■ Check for tannin staining.
■ Look for signs of restoration — differences in tone — particularly in the white areas. This may discolour with time.
■ An early set of 12 should have two bread plates. Later sets include cake plates and smaller plates.
■ If there are more than six pieces available, it is worth buying any extras the shop might have in case of damage later.
■ Where the mark includes the word *England*, the piece was probably made after 1891.

Slop bowls are today often mistaken for sugar bowls. They were, in fact, the receptacle into which the dregs of the first cup of tea were emptied.

Cream Jugs and Cow Creamers

As tea-drinking increased in popularity through the 18th and 19th centuries, it led to the production of a huge variety of jugs and creamers

When, in the mid-18th century, it first became fashionable to take milk or cream with tea, the infant British ceramics industry set about producing jugs for serving it. The first models made were very much imitations of the silverware available at the time, but among the innumerable later styles that developed was a peculiar type of vessel in the shape of a dairy cow.

Cow creamers, as they became known, had a looped-over tail to form a handle and a lowing, open mouth which served as a spout. The hollow belly of the cow could hold up to a quarter of a pint of milk and was filled via a lidded hole in the animal's back. Cow creamers began as a broad joke, but became a popular folk object, found in every type of ware and colour. Their shape made them difficult to clean and they were soon deemed too impractical for regular use. Nevertheless they survived into Edwardian

COMPARISONS

Silver Helmet Jug

SILVER CREAM JUGS FIRST APPEARED AFTER 1700. IN THE LAST QUARTER OF THE 18TH CENTURY, THE TASTE FOR NEOCLASSICAL DESIGN BROUGHT THE HELMET SHAPE INTO FASHION.

times, still popular for their decorative charm which brought them a place on many a festive table.

EARLY JUGS

Cream jugs, on the other hand, were an integral part of most tea services from around 1800 onwards and the huge scope on offer to collectors leads most to concentrate on, apart from the earliest pottery wares, the finer materials, namely silver, bone china and porcelain. When milk or cream was first taken with tea it was

brought to the table hot. Jugs were as a result usually made of silver which, in the absence of porcelain, was commonly used for hot liquids such as tea and coffee. The first silver jugs were tall and gilt-lined with a wide lip for pouring, standing either on a broad foot or on three small legs. Later in the 18th century, as the fashion for hot milk declined, cream boats, similar in shape to sauce boats, were introduced.

As tea-drinking spread to the masses in the growing new towns, the porcelain factories and potteries began to produce their own versions of the jugs, copying the silver styles. Some were made with less generous lips – the sparrow-beak jug was tall and shapely with a sharp-angled lip – but generally the basic shape remained the same, adopting the broad foot rather than the charming but all-too-breakable three-legged version.

By Edwardian times most decorative styles of the previous two centuries were available in several versions, from the cheap pottery jug to the specially commissioned hand-painted Minton porcelain.

A LIMITED HEYDAY

Once introduced, cream jugs were definitely here to stay, whereas cow creamers enjoyed a long but limited heyday. After being at their height of popularity between about 1770 and 1870, by the early 20th century they had really fallen out of daily use. Crude versions of cow creamers continued to be produced but these were bought simply as novelties and ornaments.

The real origin of cow creamers in Britain is still surrounded by uncertainty. It is thought that they were actually a Dutch invention and their arrival in Britain around

◄ Today's cream jug collectors have an enormous variety of shapes and materials to draw from. Cow creamers offer similar possibilities as the output from potteries all over Britain was truly prolific and many distinctive local styles emerged over the centuries.

▲ The Worcester factory produced the first successful blue underglaze transfer-printing around the mid-18th century. Two cream jugs of the period are shown here – the left-hand example has a typical Rococo handle.

1750 is attributed to one or other of two Dutch silversmiths based in London. Johann Schuppe and David Willaume the Younger are variously supposed to have inspired the potters with scrupulously modelled, free-standing silver cow creamers which had hinged lids in the form of a pad of flowers and a bee as a knop. But this theory is not uncontested – the City Museum at Hanley, Stoke on Trent, which has an impressive collection of 666 creamers has a ceramic example from Stoke reputed to date from 1740.

PROLIFIC OUTPUT

Some of the finest early creamers are attributed to Thomas Whieldon, whose experiments in the 1760s in mixing different-coloured clays under clear glazes produced the tortoiseshell effect known as agate ware. Others are attributed to William Pratt of Lane Delph, the originator of the style known as Prattware. His cow creamers are marked by characteristic high-temperature colours fired under a bright, glassy glaze.

Apart from Pratt and Whieldon, and a few other reputed potters such as Obadiah Sherratt, the majority of cow creamer potters were little-known, working in Wales, Scotland, and the north and west of England, as well as around Stoke.

They produced millions of colourful cows – and occasionally, joke upon joke, a rare bull creamer – until the middle of the 19th century. Impossible to clean effectively, cow creamers were responsible for several outbreaks of salmonella poisoning, but it was the new respect for hygiene brought about by the cholera scares of the 1850s that retired them to the quieter pastures of the mantelshelf or the kitchen dresser.

Cream Jugs

Cream-jug shapes went swiftly in and out of fashion in the 18th and 19th centuries, but the underlying trend was away from tall, slender jugs towards wider, shorter designs. By the beginning of the Edwardian period, simpler decorations were gaining ground over the ornate, elaborate classicism of high Victorian taste, but a wide range of decorative styles was still available to buyers.

The best wares in bone china or true, hard-paste porcelain were hand-painted with flowers and fruit in a compendium of designs, ranging from the Japanese taste through continental styles to the pure Englishness of Royal Worcester or Crown Derby. These, along with Minton, Copeland and Royal Doulton, were the leading manufacturers of the era.

All good wares from this period are clearly marked with the date, factory, and, in the case of the most exclusive, with the retailer. Some hand-painted pieces are also signed by their decorators, which adds appreciably to their value.

▼ *The Victorians often drew on earlier styles. This white porcelain jug with spreading foot (c.1880) is reminiscent of the 18th-century baluster shape.*

PRICE GUIDE **2**

▶ *Metallic lustre glazes were used on earthenware and bone china from the early 19th century onwards. This mid-Victorian Staffordshire jug has a copper lustre band above a hand-painted enamel design on sky blue ground.*

PRICE GUIDE **3**

▼ *An unusual majolica cream jug moulded to resemble a cauliflower. Minton produced a huge range of quality majolica wares between 1851-62. These were soon imitated by a host of lesser potters.*

PRICE GUIDE **5**

▲ *The low, boat shape was typical of many early 19th-century jugs. This Wedgwood jug, dated 1810, is an example of the 'fish roe' pattern. The handle is damaged and this has reduced the value.*

PRICE GUIDE **3**

PRICE GUIDE

▶ *High-handled, broad-spouted porcelain cream jug dated c.1840. The small feet characteristic of many Victorian jugs were derived from earlier 18th-century silver examples. This one is decorated with elaborate gilded patterning.*

PRICE GUIDE 2

▼ *Unusual abstract-patterned cream jug with mauve transfer-printed design, highlighted with trailing lines of lustre. The jug is unmarked but is quite likely mid-Victorian.*

PRICE GUIDE 3

▲ *A miniature version of the popular octagonal Mason's Ironstone jug (these were made in a graduated range of sizes). This example shows the Japanese-influenced Imari pattern, painted in characteristically rich colours.*

PRICE GUIDE 4

◀ *Early Victorian porcelain cream jug which follows the contemporary sauce-boat shape. Chinese patterns and oriental designs in general, came in and out of fashion throughout the 19th century.*

PRICE GUIDE 3

PRICE GUIDE

Cow Creamers

Collectable cow creamers date from 1750 to 1850. They are hardly ever marked and can rarely be attributed to a particular potter. The basic design barely changed and the main variation is in details of the bases and in the glazes. Most came from potteries centred in Staffordshire or Wales.

Staffordshire cow creamers were made in salt-glazed stoneware, earthenware, cream ware, jet-black Jackfield ware, bone china, agate ware or pearl ware; the commonest finish was a tan glaze dappled with blue, green, black, orange or yellow, though lustre glazes were also used. The cow's tail curves on to its back and the elliptical bases are usually green.

Early Welsh examples are in splashed lustre ware, but later examples have transfer-printed rural scenes on both sides and sometimes the base as well (which may be oval or oblong). The tail curving on to the flank is another characteristic feature. Yorkshire cows have waisted oblong bases with chamfered corners, and many have their eyes outlined in blue. The Sunderland factory made colourful lustre creamers until it closed down in 1878. Other potteries in Scotland and the west of England turned out yet more naive work, still appealing to today's collectors.

▶ *Black cow creamer with gold lustre spots. The straight horns set on to the sides of the head give it an unusual appearance while the low tail position makes it awkward to pick up.*

PRICE GUIDE ❹

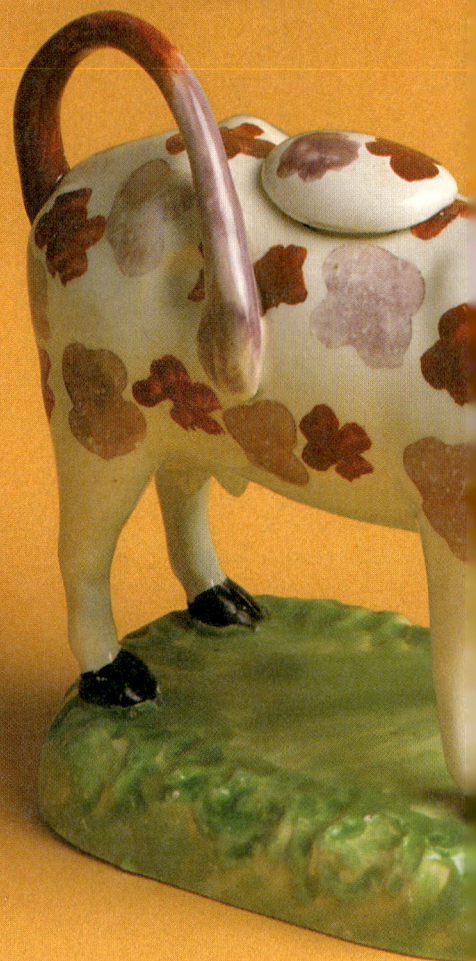

◀ *Staffordshire creamer c.1800, on small, square-ended base. The head, body and lid are covered with a haphazard iron-red and black clover-leaf pattern which would have been applied with a sponge prior to glazing.*

PRICE GUIDE ❻

PRICE GUIDE

◄ *Like the model below, this creamer (c. 1800) is recognizably a Sunderland model with its random daubs of rust and lilac lustre. Other variations combined pink or lilac with blue or green.*

PRICE GUIDE **5**

▼ *The only naturalistically coloured cows were attempts at reproducing the Herefordshire breed. This example, dated 1870, and with its squat, stout build, is also very realistic in its modelling.*

PRICE GUIDE **5**

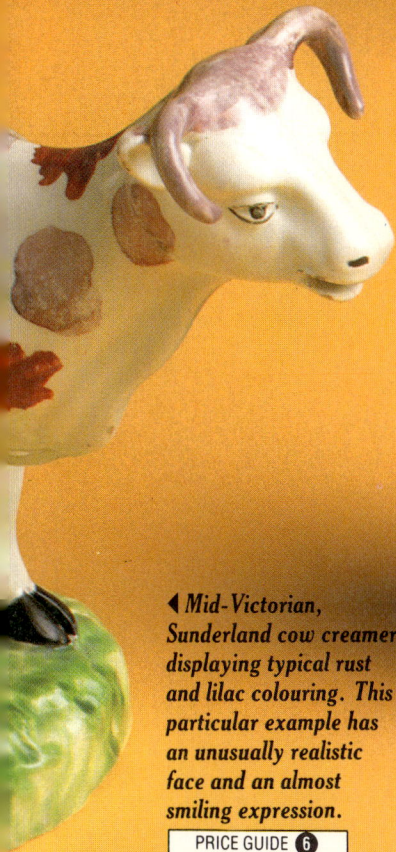

◄ *Mid-Victorian, Sunderland cow creamer displaying typical rust and lilac colouring. This particular example has an unusually realistic face and an almost smiling expression.*

PRICE GUIDE **6**

◄ *19th-century black Staffordshire creamer. Cows of this type are sometimes erroneously called 'Jackfield'. Original Jackfield cows were produced in Shropshire (1750-75) but much reproduced since.*

PRICE GUIDE **5**

PRICE GUIDE

COLLECTOR'S TIPS

The sheer quantity of wares available from the late Victorian and Edwardian eras makes creating a collection of cream jugs an accessible proposition. Most collectors prefer to specialize in wares from one factory, or to amass whole services, but since so many have already been split up, there is plenty of scope for collecting one particular item from a service and so cover a wide range of styles and factories.

Cream jugs in perfect condition can span a wide price range. A simple jug with printed decoration will be the cheapest to buy; good quality modelling and attractive hand-painting obviously add value, as does a signature. Crown Derby and Royal Worcester, especially blush ivory, command higher prices than other factories. Art Nouveau work by continental makers such as Rosenthal, Rosenburg, or the Limoges or Royal Copenhagen factories, particularly with jewelled porcelain or pierced decoration, can be very expensive.

COW PRICES

Cow creamers, belonging as many of them do to the early years of the British ceramics industry, can command extremely high prices, and the rare examples are rising all the time. Age is a big factor but generally price depends more on the complexity of the models, the neatness of the potting, the quality and gaiety of the glazes, and the overall charm of the piece.

Anything that adds to the individuality of the creamer will increase its value. Sometimes the cow is kept company by a calf, either suckling or lying at its feet. Sometimes there is a milkmaid, often made wildy out of scale and sitting beneath the animal rather than beside it. A milkmaid or a calf can add

Silver or Mock-Silver?

LUSTRE GLAZES COULD LOOK VERY LIKE THE REAL THING: THE JUG ON THE LEFT IS IN FACT MADE OF EARTHENWARE, COATED WITH A PLATINUM-OXIDE GLAZE. ALL-OVER SILVER LUSTRE, OR 'POOR MAN'S SILVER', WAS MADE IN CONSIDERABLE QUANTITY UP TO 1840, PARTICULARLY IN SUNDERLAND.

Staffordshire Cow Creamers

THE STAFFORDSHIRE POTTERIES WERE AMONG THE MAJOR PRODUCERS OF COW CREAMERS IN THE 19TH CENTURY AND THE MAJORITY OF RUN-OF-THE-MILL EXAMPLES FOUND IN ANTIQUE SHOPS TODAY WILL MORE THAN LIKELY ORIGINATE FROM THE STAFFORDSHIRE AREA. EARLY EXAMPLES HAD THIN RECTANGULAR BASES, BUT LATER COWS STAND ON HEAVIER, OVAL ONES, SOMETIMES DECORATED WITH A LARGE MOULDED DAISY OR A BUTTER PAT.

WITH THEIR TYPICAL BLACK, BROWN AND GREEN SHADES OF COLOURING, MANY OF THE COWS PRODUCED IN STAFFORDSHIRE ACTUALLY BEAR CLOSE RESEMBLANCE TO THE FLAT-BACK FIGURES, ESPECIALLY THOSE WHICH FEATURE A STANDING FIGURE. LIKE THE FLAT-BACKS, DETAIL AND DECORATION WAS CONFINED TO THE FRONT AND SIDES OF THESE FIGURES. MANY WERE NEVER USED AS CREAMERS, BUT WERE PLACED IN DAIRY WINDOWS AS AN ADVERTISEMENT.

① CROOKED ARM OF FIGURE SERVES AS HANDLE IN PLACE OF THE TAIL

② HOLE IN TOP OF HAT PROVIDES OPENING FOR CREAM

③ THE REVERSE OF COW IS SMOOTH AND FEATURELESS LIKE A FLAT-BACK

④ NEARSIDE LEGS ARE EXTREMELY FINELY MODELLED

·CLOSE UP·

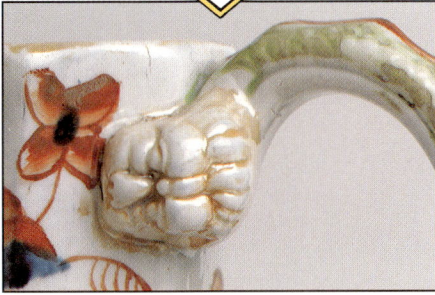

① **HYDRA HANDLE**

① A GREEN AND BROWN GLAZED HANDLE IN THE FORM OF THE HYDRA SEA-SNAKE IS TYPICAL OF MASON'S IRONSTONE JUGS. EVEN ON THIS JUG THE FEATURES ARE CLEAR.

④ THIS 19TH-CENTURY COW OWES ITS REALISTIC APPEARANCE TO ITS CAREFUL PAINTING IN NATURAL-LOOKING COLOURS.

② **RIVET REPAIR**

② RIVETS ARE AN OUT-DATED AND UNSIGHTLY METHOD OF REPAIR. ANY DAMAGE AFFECTS VALUE BUT PROFESSIONAL RESTORERS MAKE REPAIRS ALMOST INVISIBLE.

⑤ THE SMALL LIDDED HOLES IN THE COWS' BACKS MADE THEM DIFFICULT TO CLEAN. NON-MATCHING LIDS LOWER VALUE.

③ **PAINTED FLOWERS**

③ PANELS OF SPRIGGED FLOWERS, OUTLINED WITH SCROLLED ROCOCO-STYLE GILDING. THE TEXTURE OF THE DESIGN AND COLOUR BLENDING INDICATE HAND PAINTING.

⑥ VERY CRUDE MODELLING WAS A FEATURE OF THE MAJORITY OF COW CREAMERS, BUT IN MANY CASES, IT ONLY ADDS TO THE APPEAL.

④ **REALISTIC CREAMER**

⑤ **LIDDED OPENING**

⑥ **NAIVE MODELLING**

50 to 100 per cent to the price of a cow creamer.

Other details that can considerably enhance prices are a recognizable daisy, a milk pail, kicking straps (the tether put on the hind legs of a cow being milked to stop it upsetting the pail), a bell around the cow's neck, or anything that gives the animal a personality; an expressively-painted face, a head turned to one side, or a crumpled horn (except where it is the result of an inelegant repair). A neat, well-made base and an original stopper – (especially one with a moulded knop) can also make a difference.

Lack of a stopper, or its replacement with one that is not original, is a common cause of devaluation. The horns, too, are particularly vulnerable to breakage and their loss detracts both from the cow's appearance and value.

FAMOUS NAMES
Creamers dating from the 1760s and 70s and definitely attributable to Whieldon or Pratt are museum pieces. Whieldon's work

was thin and easily damaged and is now so rare that a single creamer could go for thousands. Eighteenth-century work in the Pratt style is highly sought-after especially if there is a calf or milkmaid.

Simple Staffordshire cows are the most run-of-the-mill but can be surprisingly expensive to buy. Look out for jet-black Jackfield cows, with their gilded horns and hooves, but make sure that they are authentic as many have been reproductions of these.

Occasionally a porcelain piece comes on the market, either from the continent or from one of a handful of British factories like Copeland. Copeland creamers are immediately recognizable by the way the base is scalloped up into a central pillar that helps to support the cow's stomach but does nothing for the naturalism of the pose. Porcelain examples, although rare, do not interest collectors as much as pottery.

POINTS TO WATCH
■ Heavy gilding on horns or hooves may

attempt to conceal a repair of some kind.
■ Pieces with no bases are invariably recent, and of little value.
■ Genuine old lustre ware is mottled pink in a gentle light, but shows up gold in the sunlight or under a strong bulb.
■ Early pieces made before 1830 are roughly finished inside.

▲ *The unusual design of this Regency china cream jug gives it a spout instead of a lip, giving a tea pot-like appearance.*

Blue and White China

The development of the new technique of transfer printing
revolutionized the pottery industry, leading to the mass production of
attractively decorated blue and white china

With its amazingly varied and often lavishly printed designs, 'blue and white' was admired by people of all classes in early Victorian Britain. While those 'upstairs' might eat off transfer-printed porcelain, cheaper pottery versions of blue and white could equally well be found on the dresser shelves in the servants' hall, their oriental scenes and romantic views bringing a curiously exotic note into that usually drab, toilsome environment.

ORIENTAL ORIGINS

This ware originated as a substitute for hand-painted Chinese blue and white porcelain, which enjoyed an unsurpassed prestige from the time it was first seen in Europe in the 17th century. Although Chinese porcelain was imported into Britain over a long period, only a wealthy minority could afford it, and even they were daunted by the difficulty of replacing damaged and lost items. There was clearly a large potential market for a similar product, if it could be made less expensively and closer to home. Economical mass production became possible when it was discovered that printed designs could be transferred on to ceramics, saving greatly on the cost of hand-painting.

The new process of transfer printing, invented in an enamel factory, was employed in the 1750s at the Bow porcelain works, and originally designs were printed in black. It was soon found that more successful results could be obtained using blue cobalt oxide and the technique quickly spread to Worcester and Caughley in Shropshire. By the 1780s the Staffordshire potters Josiah Spode and Thomas Minton were applying it to the cheaper earthen-ware, and a few years later Spode also perfected bone china, the form of earthen-ware best suited to transfer printing. By the early 19th century the worst technical difficulties had been overcome, and after the end of the long Napoleonic wars in 1815 the manufacture of transfer-printed wares became a major British industry with a profitable export trade focused on the United States, for which plates were specially decorated with American scenes.

COMPARISONS

Eastern Influences

A 17TH-CENTURY CHINESE PLATE MADE
FOR THE EXPORT TRADE. BRITISH BLUE
AND WHITE CHINA INITIALLY
IMITATED ORIENTAL PORCELAIN.

The basic technique of transfer printing began with the making of an engraving. Special tools were used to cut the required design into a copper plate and by cutting to various depths and employing lines and dots for shadings, the practised engraver could achieve subtle tonal variations and an extremely high degree of artistry. The engraved plate was covered with warm oily blue ink, then wiped over very thoroughly, so that the colour remained only in the engraved areas below the surface. When pressed on to a sheet of paper, the plate printed the design. The engraving process had been used for centuries to make prints and book illustrations, but its application to ceramics was new. The paper used for transfer printing on china was tissue paper coated with size – a soapy substance that prevented the design from sinking in. The printed tissue paper was placed on the ceramic body, which had been hardened by a preliminary firing, and then rubbed down

▶ *A delicate blue and white tea set was an essential part of the ritual of afternoon tea. The cups and saucers and teapot are decorated with flowers and birds: they are typical of the teawares produced by potteries all over Britain in the mid-19th century.*

◀ *A collection of 19th-century blue and white china is the perfect addition to an antique pine dresser. The pieces may not match, but the diversity adds interest rather than detracting from the total effect, and the various shades of soft blue blend well with each other.*

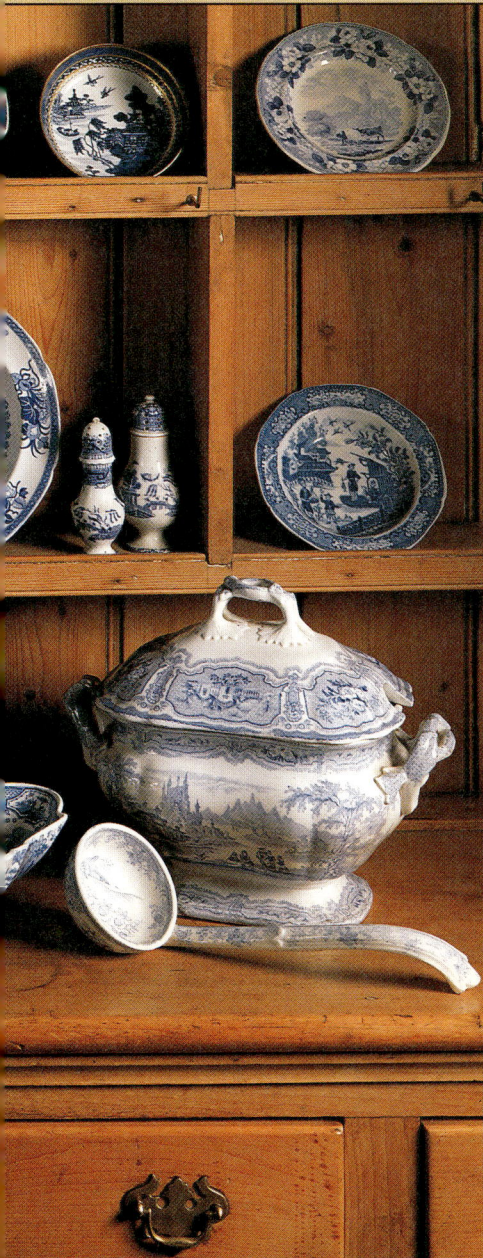

with a brush to transfer the design. The paper was then sponged away and the object dipped in a fluid glaze which hardened to a thin, transparent protective film. A second firing created the hard-wearing and highly decorative final object.

THE PRINTING SHOP
The manufacture of transfer-printed china involved many separate processes; those carried out in the printing shop were the most complicated and important, and were always performed by hand. We catch a glimpse of the printing shop in Arnold Bennett's novel *Anna of the Five Towns* when Anna is taken on a tour of her fiancé's 'model three-oven bank'. She eventually reaches a room that 'smelt of oil and flannel and humanity', where 'by means of copper-plates, printing presses, mineral colours, and transfer-papers, most of the decoration was done. The room was filled by a little crowd of people – oldish men, women and girls, divided into printers, cutters, transfer-rers and apprentices. Each interminably repeated some trifling process, and every article passed through a succession of hands until at length it was washed in a tank and rose dripping therefrom with its ornament of flowers and scrolls fully revealed.'

ROMANTIC ASSOCIATIONS
Until about 1820, transfer-printed ware was of necessity blue and white, since blue was the only colour that could be success-fully printed under the glaze. However, the predominance of blue and white outlived this purely technical advantage, since it was based on the association with the colour scheme of Chinese porcelain. Up to about 1800 the decoration of English blue and white was emphatically 'Oriental', consist-ing either of direct copies of Chinese landscapes or adaptations *(chinoiseries)* that suited romanticized Western notions of the Far East. The most famous of these was the Willow pattern, which many people believe to be Chinese, although both the pattern and the touching story of star-crossed lovers it depicts are Western inventions.

FAVOURITE THEMES
'Chinese' blue and white remained popular into Victorian times but it was gradually superseded by a considerable vogue for picturesque British views and foreign scenes, mostly taken directly from engraved prints and book illustrations, which were not protected by copyright until 1842.

However, not all compositions were copied. As early as the 1830s, many ceramic artists were producing their own original designs, which were often imaginary scenes with vague suggestions of a romantic setting such as Venice or the Alps. The most common were landscapes with ruins, lakes, bridges, boats and other picturesque features, and despite their fanciful and naive look, many were charming and skilfully executed. These, or standard designs such as the Willow pattern or the floral 'Asiatic Pheasants', were used in the dining room and the servants' hall alike until the late 1850s when quality declined, fashions changed, and transfer printing was reduced to a cheap means of applying floral decoration to china.

Dinner Ware

The most commonly found English blue and white china is dinner ware, which was produced in vast quantities during the 19th century. A full dinner service for a wealthy household constituted an imposing array of different plates for soup, the main course and puddings, as well as meat and vegetable dishes, tureens, sauce boats and other items. Side plates for bread and butter were not normally included, but there were often twice as many dinner plates as other pieces, which is probably why many have survived.

Such services reflect the extraordinary variety of subject-matter that was drawn on for the decoration of transfer-printed wares. The more or less flat surfaces of plates made them particularly suitable for landscape views, and diners appear to have been equally happy to gaze down on Wedgwood's crowded *Blue Bamboo* pattern or the melancholy romanticism of Ridgeway's *Tomb of Kosciuso*. In some services each item was decorated with a separate scene or pattern, so that over 50 different engravings could be made for a single service. Others, such as Spode's *Blue Italian* displayed the same view on each piece. However, the borders on items such as plates were always identical, providing the service with a unifying element.

By the 1830s plate patterns were becoming less dense, and a white undecorated area usually separated the central design from the border. Later in the century a more radical change in fashion undermined the popularity of blue-printed designs, since plates were manufactured with brightly coloured borders and otherwise left undecorated.

▲ Dinner plates from the 'British History' series by Jones & Sons, depicting the signing of the Magna Carta. It dates from 1827.

PRICE GUIDE ④

▲ Spode soup plate with an ironstone body called 'New Stone', which was introduced by the company early in the 1820s.

PRICE GUIDE ③

▲ An attractive vegetable dish with a lion handle, made by a Staffordshire pottery c.1830. It is decorated with scenes of the countryside.

PRICE GUIDE ⑤

▶ Small tureen from around 1820, with a lattice pattern and speckled handles. Its size suggests that it was used for serving sauces.

PRICE GUIDE ⑤

▲ Creamer, used for pouring milk or cream, decorated with an unidentified floral pattern and landscape scenes.

PRICE GUIDE ④

PRICE GUIDE

◀ The bowl of this ladle is decorated with an oriental scene showing temples and a pagoda. It dates from c.1850.

PRICE GUIDE 3

▲ Meat platter in Spode 'Stone China' dating from 1820. It is decorated with the Grasshopper pattern.

PRICE GUIDE 5

◀ A small ladle from the mid-19th century, probably used for sauces. It has a floral design and a silver band on the handle.

PRICE GUIDE 3

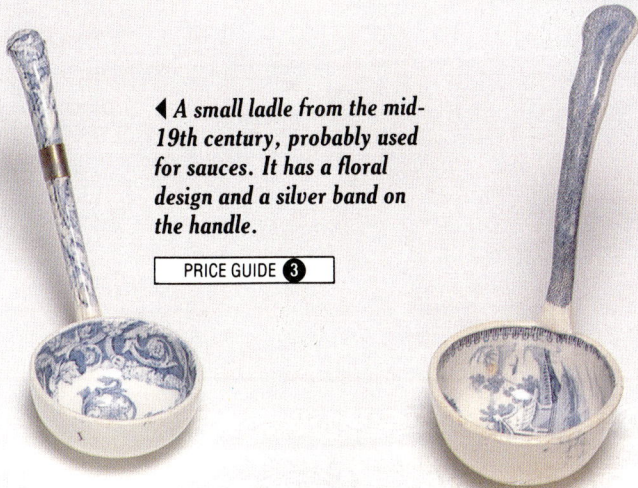

▲ Minton soup plate dating from 1820. The pattern is 'Mandarin', and it features several diminutive Chinese figures.

PRICE GUIDE 5

◀ A large salad bowl made by an unidentified Staffordshire potter in the mid-1820s. The pattern shows a ruined temple and pyramid set in a landscape.

PRICE GUIDE 5

PRICE GUIDE

Tea and Coffee Sets

Although the majority of surviving transfer-printed wares originally belonged to dinner services, many other kinds were manufactured including tea and coffee sets. Tea-drinking gained in popularity following the reduction of tax on tea from 119 per cent to 12½ per cent in 1784, and this stimulated demand for teawares. But extensive use led to a high casualty rate for cups and saucers, so that a surprisingly small number survive intact.

The basic cup-and-saucer set was economically manufactured as what is now known as a trio, serving both popular beverages; the set consisted of a tea-cup, a coffee-cup (or 'can'), and a single saucer which could be used with either.

Apart from the pouring pots, tea and coffee sets offered rather unsuitable surfaces for some of the more elaborate scenic designs, and therefore carried a more restricted range of decoration than plates and other dinnerwares. Floral patterns were particularly common, but could be strikingly original as well as of high quality; a notable example is a mid-19th century Minton set with elegantly formal, stylized Gothic decoration by the distinguished architect A.W.N. Pugin.

Transfer printing was also employed on other pieces that would have been found on the tea table, such as cake stands, sugar bowls, milk jugs, slop bowls and tea plates.

◀ *A comport used for cakes or fruit, decorated with an attractive chintz pattern and showing traces of a gold-painted rim.*

PRICE GUIDE ④

▲ *Slop bowl with an oriental-inspired abstract design inside the rim, and a peacock on the outside.*

PRICE GUIDE ③

▲ *Sugar bowl with deep blue floral decoration and a scalloped edge, dating from the mid-1820s.*

PRICE GUIDE ⑤

▲ *Early Victorian tea-cup and saucer with a typical rustic scene of fishermen in front of a cottage, and a floral border.*

PRICE GUIDE ③

▶ *A 'Breadalbane' tea plate with a plaid border, depicting a castle set in a Scottish landscape, complete with mountain peaks and a loch.*

PRICE GUIDE ③

PRICE GUIDE

▲ *A low comport with two handles for teatime dainties. The leaf decoration is particularly unusual.*

PRICE GUIDE **4**

▼ *Teapot from the 1820s, with a design depicting three children playing. The lid has been repaired.*

PRICE GUIDE **5**

▲ *A teapot with a rare shape dating from around 1800. It is decorated with a Chinese-inspired pattern.*

PRICE GUIDE **5**

◄ *A creamer with a pattern of flowers, leaves and scrolls.*

PRICE GUIDE **4**

◄ *Tea plate from 1830, decorated with a dark blue design showing an idyllic country scene with boats and fishermen.*

PRICE GUIDE **3**

▲ *Plate made by the Don pottery in Yorkshire around 1820, with cows grazing in English pastures.*

PRICE GUIDE **5**

PRICE GUIDE

COLLECTOR'S TIPS

Transfer-printed wares were produced all over Britain and in vast quantities. They were designed to attract several different income groups and were therefore made in different materials and decorated with varying degrees of skill and sophistication. All this makes the subject of blue and white a complicated one, and the wealth of

The Trio

TEA AND COFFEE SETS WERE OFTEN PRODUCED IN THE FORM OF A 'TRIO' CONSISTING OF ONE SAUCER, A TEA-CUP AND A COFFEE CUP.

specialist books and articles – not to mention the existence of a Friends of Blue Club for the committed – mean that the prospective collector should be prepared to invest some time in study before plunging into the market for wares that are by no means cheap. However, there is abundant information available to the real enthusiast which will help him overcome difficulties of judgement and identification.

Almost every one of the numerous pottery firms in Staffordshire – the heart of the industry – manufactured transfer-printed blue and white. So did firms all over the United Kingdom: Bow in London, the Worcester works, Caughley in Shropshire and Lowestoft in Suffolk played an important part in the early history of blue and white, but in the boom years Swansea, Liverpool, Leeds, Sheffield, Newcastle upon Tyne and many other towns became centres of manufacture. The host of factories in Staffordshire included well-known names such as New Hall, Davenport and

Minton, but the foremost firm was undoubtedly Spode of Stoke-on-Trent, both for its technical contribution and the sheer quality of its products. These are clearly marked, and the firm's changes of name (it became Copeland & Garrett in 1833, and W.T. Copeland in 1847) provide an instant means of dating a piece to within a few decades.

USEFUL MARKS

Other wares can also be helpfully marked, especially those on which the underside carries a backstamp – a decorative mark giving the name of the printed scene or design and including the maker's initials and the trade name of the materials from which the piece was made. But many other pieces of blue and white are unmarked, and attempts to identify them by characteristic features are often frustrated by the fact that the same patterns were frequently used by two or more firms (one popular border, the *Wild Rose*, actually appeared on different

The Supper Set

THE STRANGE FAN-SHAPED DISHES THAT OCCASIONALLY TURN UP IN ANTIQUE SHOPS WERE ONCE PART OF SUPPER SETS, DESIGNED TO HOLD LATE-NIGHT SNACKS TO WHICH THE MASTER AND THE MISTRESS OF THE HOUSE WOULD HELP THEMSELVES AFTER THE SERVANTS HAD RETIRED TO BED. COMPLETE SETS — NOW RARELY FOUND — CONSISTED OF FOUR COVERED DISHES AND A CENTRAL TUREEN, WHICH WAS USED EITHER TO CONTAIN A SAUCE, OR FOR BOILED EGGS. SOME

TUREENS WERE FITTED OUT WITH A RACK HOLDING FOUR OR SIX EGGCUPS AND A SALT CELLAR. THE WHOLE SET WAS PRESENTED ON ITS OWN CIRCULAR OR ELLIPTICAL WOODEN TRAY.

SUPPER SETS WERE MADE BY MANY POTTERS INCLUDING WILLIAM ADAMS, WEDGWOOD AND SPODE, BUT THE MAKER OF THIS PARTICULAR VICTORIAN EXAMPLE HAS NOT BEEN IDENTIFIED. THE DECORATION IS THE WILLOW PATTERN.

① THE TWO END SECTIONS STILL HAVE THEIR LIDS, BUT THESE SEEM TO BE MISSING FROM THE OTHER TWO DISHES.

② THE TUREEN LID HAS BEEN REPAIRED, AND ONE DISH IS CHIPPED. THE PRICE SHOULD REFLECT THIS.

③ WILLOW PATTERN IS NOT AN EASY AID TO IDENTIFICATION, AS IT WAS MADE BY SO MANY DIFFERENT POTTERS, WHO EACH ADDED THEIR OWN VARIATIONS TO THE PATTERN.

·CLOSE UP·

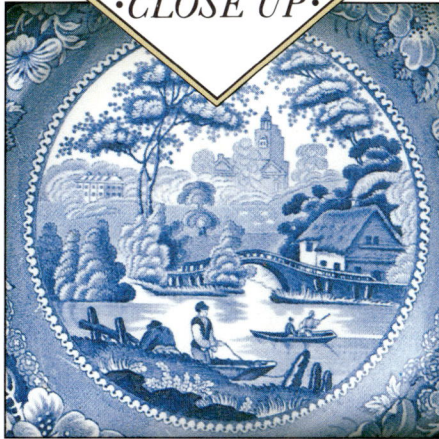

① **RUSTIC SCENE**

② **PICTURESQUE MOTIF**

③ **PRINTED MARK**

④ **MISMATCHED PATTERNS**

⑤ **OVERLAPPING AREAS**

⑥ **IRONSTONE CHINA**

① A TYPICALLY ROMANTICIZED VIEW OF THE BRITISH COUNTRYSIDE.

② CASTLES, STATELY HOMES AND OTHER PICTURESQUE BUILDINGS ARE OFTEN THE FOCUS OF A DESIGN.

③ BACKS OF PLATES OFTEN CARRY SERIES AND MAKERS' MARKS.

④ MISMATCHED PATTERNS SOMETIMES INDICATE WHERE ONE TRANSFER BEGINS AND ANOTHER ENDS.

⑤ HERE THE MAIN AREA OF DECORATION OVERLAPS THE BORDER.

⑥ IRONSTONE – HEAVY EARTHENWARE CONTAINING SLAG – OFTEN HAD BLUE AND WHITE DECORATION.

wares from a dozen different factories!)

Subject matter can offer a useful provisional dating: a topographical view is likely to have originated between about 1800 and 1835, whereas a non-oriental fantasy ('romantic') landscape probably belongs to the 1830s or later. But, given the vagaries and inconsistencies of manufacturers and fashions, this is hardly to be relied on in the absence of other supporting evidence. Different catalogues of patterns in the specialist literature will almost certainly prove helpful in placing any item the collector comes across, even if no definite conclusions can be reached.

FINE QUALITY

Quality is in the eye of the beholder, and most collectors sensibly prefer to buy what pleases them rather than follow rules laid down by other people. But in terms of financial value, fineness of detail and variety of tone in the decoration are fairly obvious criteria that are likely to be important.

Early transfer printing produced a dark cobalt; later the colour became lighter and more detail was achieved. Although early on there was almost always a faint blurring, the dark blue of early pieces should not be confused with the flow blue that became especially popular in export wares from the late 1830s, in which the diffusion of the blue into the glaze was deliberately contrived by placing certain chemicals in the kiln before firing to produce a blurred image.

POINTS TO WATCH

■ Damage or obvious repairs will seriously detract from the value of a piece.
■ Attribution can be difficult because patterns originated by one manufacturer were often copied by another, and many pieces are unmarked.
■ Complete dinner and tea services are rarely found, but unmatched pieces can look effective displayed together on a dresser or on the wall.

▲ *A jug for milk or water dating from about 1850 in the Humphrey's Clock pattern, and decorated with an idealized rural scene complete with gnarled tree and church spire.*

The Ewer and Basin

Functional as well as decorative, the china ewer and basin was an indispensable addition to any Edwardian lady's boudoir

China toilet sets took pride of place in the Edwardian lady's bedroom. Even though bathrooms were a more or less established feature of larger houses, the ewer and basin was still found on the marble washstand in the boudoir. Ladies preferred to cleanse themselves in the privacy of their own bedroom and, with a personal maid at their beck and call, it was easy enough to summon hot water when required. The bath was still only a weekly event and, as far as the Edwardian lady was concerned, morning and evening washing in the bedroom sufficed.

MATCHING SETS

Extensive toilet sets – some numbering as many as 30 separate pieces – were often given as a wedding present to the bride. These gifts were displayed on the washstand, which was a large marble-topped table with a splashback covered in brightly coloured tiles. The sets were treasured as replacement pieces were often hard to come by. If it were made in strong colours, the effect of a large set could be overwhelming, such as one black earthenware set, which was ornamented with roses and included vases and

The Washstand

▲ THE WASHSTAND WAS RARELY A THING OF BEAUTY, THOUGH THIS ONE HAS A COLOURFUL TILED SPLASHBACK AND A MARBLE TOP.

jardinières to adorn the pot stands that stood in every bedroom window.

The simplest toilet set consisted of a ewer, basin and covered soap dish. Cheaper soap dishes were ridged inside to allow the soap to dry, whereas the more expensive ones had a removable liner. There was also a larger sponge bowl, often with separate perforated liner to allow air to circulate. A tooth-brush holder and beaker was also part of the set, as was the chamber pot, which was kept in the bedside cabinet. A matching slop pail with wicker handle stood under the washstand ready to receive waste water.

The same china was used on the dressing table. Covered pin boxes, powder bowls and candlesticks were set out, together with the stand for holding a lady's rings and a large tray for other knick-knacks. In some of the larger sets, there were tall hatpin holders and toilet-water jugs. An object called a hair tidy matched the powder bowl, but is distinguishable by the circular hole in the lid, where the lady could dispose of loose hair from her brush and comb.

CHANGES IN STYLE

Ewers and water jugs have been used since the earliest times. In the medieval period, they were made in silver and originally used for the ritual hand washing at table after a meal. The 15th century saw the introduction of a few ceramic ewers and basins which were made of majolica and were imported from Italy. However, most of those in daily use were made of pewter or brass.

As washing became part of the daily routine – and bathrooms were still uncommon – so the ewer and basin became a feature of the bedroom. Initially they were not objects of much decorative significance until the mass production of porcelain and earthenware began in the 18th century. By this time, women who did not wash regularly had become a target of the satirists' humour. As a result, women started to take pride in displaying their sets.

The manufacture of large ewers and basins did not begin until the early years of the 19th century, when firms such as Spode, Masons and Wedgwood began to produce matching ranges in several designs and sizes. Lavishly decorated blue, red and green transfer-printed sets were the glory of this period, illustrated with buildings and everyday or heroic scenes. The hexagonal-shaped sets, made by Masons in their ironstone china in the popular 'Japan' pattern, are very typical of the period, as are the complex shell-shaped toilet dishes in pearl-like porcelain made at Beleek in Ireland.

EDWARDIAN TASTE

Plainer toilet sets became more fashionable from the last quarter of the 19th century. However, many of the popular Victorian patterned china sets continued to be produced until the 1920s, especially in the cheaper ranges. These were decorated with coloured bands or a transfer-printed spray of flowers. In general, styles became simpler and the raised decoration at the top of the ewer was abandoned in

◀ *Ladies at their toilette became a fashionable subject for painters in the late 19th century. In this painting the model was the artist's wife.*

Jug Shapes

COMPLEX HANDLES, FLUTING AND RIBBING WERE EARLY DESIGN FEATURES. BLUE AND WHITE PATTERNS WERE LIKEWISE POPULAR.

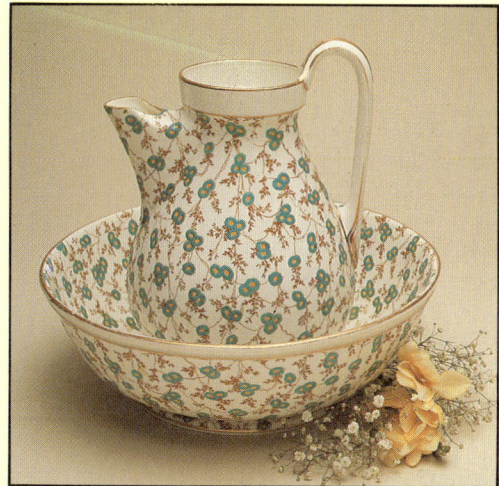

THIS ATTRACTIVELY DESIGNED TRANSFER-PRINTED SET HAS SIMPLE LINES BUT IS UNUSUAL IN HAVING A SPOUT.

CLASSICAL SIMPLICITY OF LINE AND PATTERN WAS THE HALLMARK OF LATER EDWARDIAN TOILET SETS.

China

·PRICE GUIDE·

TOILET ACCESSORIES

Matching china toilet sets are eagerly sought-after by collectors and sell for several hundred pounds but it is possible to pick up individual items for much less.

▲ *The attraction of this pine washstand, with a hole for the wash basin, lies in the practical design.*

PRICE GUIDE 5

◄ *An 1898 toilet set by Minton. It contains a ewer and basin, two candlesticks, a chamberstick, sponge dish, toothbrush holder and soap dish.*

PRICE GUIDE 7

▼ *A single ewer is worth less than one with a matching basin. In the early 1900s, a ewer and basin by Wedgwood or Minton from the Army and Navy Stores cost about a crown. A 14-piece toilet set would be three times as much.*

PRICE GUIDE 2

favour of flat surfaces, which were easier to clean. Edwardian ewers are often wide at the base, sitting fairly low in the matching basin. This practical design made them more stable and less likely to be knocked over when empty.

The trend towards plainer, more basic shapes is particularly obvious in the design of basins, which became lower and often straight-sided. Ewers sometimes imitated the traditional shapes of the tin cans used for carrying the hot water up from the kitchen. Some very functional, but well decorated sets were made by Doulton at Burslem in 1910, the wide-bellied ewer decorated with a large nightwatchman and the bowl carrying a banner with the slogan 'Watchman What of the Night'. Alongside these progressive shapes were many fluted ewers with complex handles, decorated with the sort of ornamentation that would have pleased any mid-Victorian.

THE LADY'S TOILETTE

Many ladies, recalling their Edwardian youth, commented on the vast quantities of water that were constantly carried about the house. This was to cater for the lady's morning and evening toilette in the bedroom and, if the lady enjoyed cycling, riding or tennis, she might also call for water to freshen herself during the day.

It was part of the maid's daily duty to carry great tin pitchers of hot water up the several flights of stairs from the kitchen to the bedroom. The water was kept hot as it was carried by wrapping the can with a thick towel, which could then be used by the mistress in the bedroom. Once sullied, the dirty water was

▶ *Packaged toiletries and cosmetics were big business at the turn of the century and the advertising of rival manufacturers became increasingly inventive.*

54

▲ *More unusual toilet pieces, such as this toothbrush holder, fetch surprisingly high prices today.*

PRICE GUIDE **4**

▶ *Chamber pots have long been popular with collectors, both because of their attractive decoration and their usefulness as plant pot holders.*

PRICE GUIDE **2**

▶ *This Edwardian slop pail has a lid and is made of tin, though it has been painted to have a wood finish. Dirty washing water from the basin was poured into it for subsequent disposal.*

PRICE GUIDE **5**

poured into the slop or chamber pail and the basin was rinsed out with cold water. The maid was required to empty the pail, remove the water pitcher and refill the ewer. A plain linen hand-towel was placed on the rail at the side of the washstand, while a huckaback – a coarse linen towel – was folded and placed over the ewer to keep the water dust-free. Larger turkish towels were laid across the painted or polished clothes horse which, in colder weather, stood in front of the bedroom fire.

BEAUTY AIDS

Women had become much more interested in personal hygiene and skin care, which was greatly encouraged by the exaggerated claims of contemporary advertising. With the development of cheaper printing methods towards the end of the 19th century, advertising had taken off. Large, colourful posters shouted the merits of every type of product, including the popular beauty accessories and cosmetics. Commercially made scents and skin creams featured prominently in the Edwardian toilet, with firms such as Yardley, Ponds and Pears relying heavily on advertising as well as supplying attractively packaged products. These beautifying lotions and potions were so much in vogue that even women such as Lily Langtry, mistress of the Prince of Wales

and society beauty, were happy to model for products such as Pears' soap. Competition between rival firms was so great that special coloured prints were given away when enough tokens had been collected from a product. These prints were themselves sometimes used to decorate the bedroom. The makers were also conscious of the importance of decorative pots and bottles, and Yardley, for example, sold all their scents in the Baccarat jars.

The soft soap that replaced the Victorian hard soap, at the end of the 19th century, triggered a different approach to daily washing. Quite contrary to modern beliefs, the Edwardians considered that this gentle cleanser was highly beneficial to the complexion, and so lathered it up and covered their faces completely in it. This was then rinsed off with hot water, which was ideally collected from the rain water butt outside. After this ritual at the basin, ladies sprinkled themselves liberally with scented toilet water – an important accessory in an age lacking deodorants. Cold cream was then applied to the face, along with a touch of violet powder to reduce facial colouring. Other than this, little make-up was used by respectable women, except a hint of rouge and some cherry lipsalve. However, together with the essential hair-brushing procedure, a lady's toilette could still take up to an hour to complete.

▲ *Some of the best Edwardian toilet pieces – this is a sponge dish – are decorative in any context.*

PRICE GUIDE **2**

▲ *An Edwardian soap dish with a gold rim and a popular floral design in blue and white.*

PRICE GUIDE **1**

THEN AND NOW

Lotions and Potions

EDWARDIAN TOILET PREPARATIONS WERE AVAILABLE EITHER IN PRE-PACKAGED FORM OR THEY COULD BE MADE UP BY THE LOCAL CHEMIST. MANY OF THESE ORIGINAL RECIPES HAVE BEEN REVIVED TODAY, AND SOLD IN EDWARDIAN-STYLE PACKAGING FROM NATURAL BEAUTY SHOPS.

DESPITE AVAILABILITY, MANY WOMEN CHOSE TO MAKE THEIR OWN PREPARATIONS AT HOME. SEVERAL OF THESE ORIGINAL RECIPES CAN BE FOUND IN OLD BOOKS AND BEAUTY MAGAZINES AND TRIED OUT TODAY. A CHEMIST SHOULD BE ABLE TO PROVIDE THE INGREDIENTS. FOR ROSE COLD CREAM, PLACE THE FOLLOWING IN A JAR IN THE GIVEN PROPORTIONS: SIX PARTS EACH OF OIL OF ALMONDS AND DISTILLED ROSEWATER TO ONE PART EACH OF WHITE WAX AND SPERMACETI. PLACE THE JAR IN A BOWL OF HOT WATER AND STIR UNTIL BLENDED.

Staffordshire Ornaments

Simple and unpretentious, full of naive charm, Staffordshire figures
were made for the mass market and reflected every facet of Victorian life

The ornamental figures with which the Victorians of all classes delighted in adorning their parlours have been aptly described as 'a potted history of the period'. They were a genuinely popular art, made for the mass market and dealing in the main with the same type of subjects that are now the staple diet of the tabloid newspaper. Then as now, the royal family was a source of endless fascination, and sporting heroes, stars of the stage and public figures of all kinds – famous or infamous – also featured high on the list of favourite subjects.

There was also a somewhat macabre taste for violence of the blood and thunder kind, depictions of murderers – sometimes in the act of their crimes – forming a kind of three-dimensional equivalent to the illustrated broadsheets still sold at executions of the day. Generally, however, subjects were down-to-earth, with animals and sentimental themes like homecomings and farewells being most in demand.

EVERYDAY ORNAMENTS

Staffordshire figures were bought not as the works of art they are now considered to be, but as everyday items that only the very poorest homes would have been unable to afford. Until about 1910 the cheapest figures were sold to the retail trade for just a few pence. Genteel customers would have bought them in china shops, which by the mid 19th century were common sights in the high street, but for the less well-off they were available at fairgrounds or in the numerous street markets.

An unending demand was supplied by a major industry centred on Stoke-on-Trent in Staffordshire. From the 17th century it had been the heart of the British ceramics industry (the area has long been known as 'the Potteries'), producing a vast quantity of wares, both useful and ornamental.

The production of Staffordshire figures

COMPARISONS

Meissen

THE GRACE AND ELEGANCE OF THE DELICATE FIGURES IMPORTED FROM MEISSEN, GERMANY, FORMED A DISTINCT CONTRAST WITH THE ROBUST CHARM OF STAFFORDSHIRE FIGURES.

Royal Connections

THE ROYAL FAMILY AND ALL ITS VARIOUS CONNECTIONS MAKE UP ONE OF THE LARGEST CATEGORIES OF STAFFORDSHIRE FIGURES. SEEN HERE IS VICTORIA'S SON ALFRED IN OFFICIAL DRESS AS DUKE OF EDINBURGH.

▲ *Heroic figures astride a horse or camel were a popular theme. Although often hardly accurate portraits, many figures were named while others were recognizable by their uniforms.*

◀ *Originally made as 'chimney ornaments' for the mantelpiece, Staffordshire figures today will look attractive in almost any situation. They present great scope for the collector, with subjects taken from every walk of life, from royalty to children and animals.*

began in about 1780, but their heyday was from around 1840 until the end of the century, a period coinciding almost exactly with Victoria's reign (1837-1901). There is no way of estimating how many figures were made in this time as they were manufactured in such large quantities and mostly produced anonymously – marks identifying which factory they came from are something of a rarity.

The methods used to produce Staffordshire figures were in principle quite straightforward, although the composition of the raw materials and the exact technical procedures might vary substantially – individual potters having their own jealously guarded recipes. The result of this can be seen by comparing figures produced by different factories – some are made from rough pottery, whilst others display qualities generally associated with porcelain. Very similar figures were made outside Staffordshire, notably at some Scottish potteries. Not surprisingly, given the number produced, the figures vary enormously in quality, some being extremely crude while other pieces are minor masterpieces of folk art.

The most striking characteristic of Staffordshire figures is their naive but appealing charm. Painted in bold, lively colours, they are immediately approachable, and have none of the air of mystique that is often attached to antiques. Connoisseurs might devote a lifetime to them without exhausting their fascination, but even to the uninitiated their appeal is instant.

A HISTORY IN MINIATURE

The subjects of Staffordshire figures covered the entire social spectrum, with notorious rogues and outcasts such as gipsies at one end and royalty at the other. All the most newsworthy personalities were represented in clay. In the days when colour illustrations were a rarity, such figures performed something of the function of popular magazines today. With the huge variety of identifiable characters, both real and fictional that have survived, the Staffordshire collector soon begins to build up a picture of the past.

For many people, the primary fascination of Staffordshire figures is as social history in miniature. This was the attitude of one of the greatest collectors, Henry Willett, who in 1899 wrote: 'the history of the country may to a large extent be traced on its homely pottery'. Willett left his impressive collection to the Brighton Museum and Art Gallery where it still serves as an inspiration to Staffordshire collectors today.

Popular Figures

The collector of Staffordshire figures has very wide scope for specialization. A huge range of popular figures of the day were modelled so there is something to suit virtually every taste.

Both real life celebrities and fictional characters from popular novels, theatre and opera provided great inspiration for the Staffordshire potteries. There were subjects drawn from the vivid characterizations of Charles Dickens' novels and also from the plays of Shakespeare. Figures of actors and actresses in the roles that made them famous added yet another dimension to the theatrical theme.

Military and naval heroes of the day were made in great numbers, documenting all the most important conflicts abroad. Sometimes, to keep up with topical events, simply the names on the bases of models were changed. Prime ministers and politicians of note were also represented.

In addition to celebrities, figures of simple folk in couples or groups were given particular themes of their own, with scenes such as the 'Jealous Rival', the 'Sailor's Farewell' or the 'Sailor's Return' all being interpreted by the potteries.

▶ *A rare Staffordshire figure of the Scottish love poet and lyricist, Robert Burns (1759-1896). Depicted here in a tartan shawl with a book denoting his profession, Burns was a colourful figure who appealed to the Victorians' love of all things Scottish. Other figures of Burns show him with 'Highland Mary' – supposedly Mary Campbell who was one of Burns's many loves. This carefully painted well-modelled figure would command a premium price.*

PRICE GUIDE ❻

ROBERT BURNES

PRICE GUIDE

◄ *The exoticism of travel and exploration was summed up for the Victorians in the vast range of naval figures and sailors made in Staffordshire. For ordinary sailors, the broad-brimmed hat, baggy chemise and neckerchief were typical with flags appearing during the Crimean Period.*

PRICE GUIDE **5**

► *Any sportsman who found widespread fame could expect his likeness to appear in clay. Among the sporting figures modelled were celebrity boxers in fighting pairs, also a champion jockey astride a famous mount. Cricketers, though, were some of the most popular. This figure is said to represent George Parr, an All England player.*

PRICE GUIDE **6**

▲ *Unnamed, unknown figures are generally priced lower than specifically named or identified examples. The quality of the moulding and hand-painting, however, will always add value. This well-moulded double figure of lovers has a fragile look with its thin clay umbrella and handle held in the man's hand.*

PRICE GUIDE **5**

◄ *A national heroine in her own time, Florence Nightingale (1820-1910) achieved fame as a nurse in the Crimea. Strangely, no known figure exists showing her with her famous lamp.*

PRICE GUIDE **5**

◄Opera singer Jenny Lind, much admired for the sweetness of her voice, was dubbed the 'Swedish Nightingale' after her debut in London in 1847.

PRICE GUIDE **7**

▲ Figures in rural settings were always a popular theme, especially with the many new town dwellers. Ornaments such as this pair of lovers seated beside a flowing stream were typical. This one has a tree-stump spill holder.

PRICE GUIDE **5**

▶ The dastardly murders committed by William Palmer were the subject of much macabre fascination. In two years, this outwardly benign doctor disposed of his wife, brother and friend by poisoning. The scene of the murders was his house, also reproduced.

PRICE GUIDE **7**

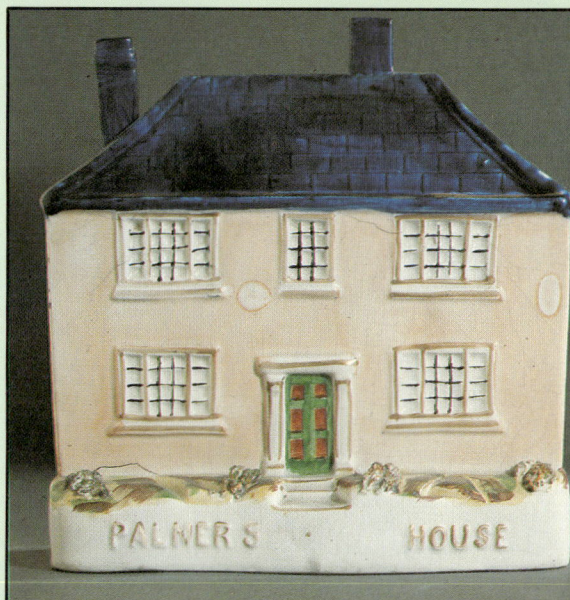

PRICE GUIDE

Animals

► *Zebras were usually made in pairs. So great was demand that moulds originally meant for horses were often used, a flowing mane being the tell-tale sign. A fascination for exotic animals was fired by the opening of the first Zoological Gardens, where animals from all over the world could be seen for the first time.*

PRICE GUIDE ❻

◄ *Pairs of King Charles spaniels were made in great numbers. This example with open front paws is of particularly fine quality.*

PRICE GUIDE ❻

► *Farm animals were also included in the Staffordshire repertoire. This pair of sheep spill holders are made in the bocage style. The realistic wool texture was created using granulated clay.*

PRICE GUIDE ❺

PRICE GUIDE

Napoleon

SIMILAR FIGURES CAN VARY QUITE SUBSTANTIALLY IN FINISH, RANGING BETWEEN VERY FINE AND RATHER CRUDE PAINTING AND MODELLING.

Napoleon Buonaparte

In recent years, Victorian Staffordshire ornaments have become highly collectable. Despite the quantity in which they were produced, some quite ordinary pieces – the sort which were sold to the masses at street markets – are now fetching large sums of money in antique shops and at auction.

The price of Staffordshire ornaments depends on both rarity and quality. Some figures and animals were turned out in such vast quantities that, although they may be attractive, they are worth substantially less than a cruder, yet rarer model. Truly fine pieces always command premium prices. Surprisingly, the earlier figures and animals were often of a much higher standard than later models.

METHODS OF PRODUCTION

The manufacture of Staffordshire ornaments began with a modeller who made an original figure out of clay. From the modeller's figure a master mould was made, and from this, in turn, further working moulds were produced. The moulds were made in two halves – front and back – and the clay for the figure was pressed quite thinly into each one. The halves were then bound tightly together and placed into the kiln for firing. Once fired, the hollow figure was removed from the mould ready for painting.

The number of figures that could be taken from each mould varied from about 20 to 200, but towards the end of each run there was an increased blurring of detail as the moulds became worn. As a result, some of the later figures in a run were sometimes not of such good quality as the first.

The principal colour used to paint the figures in the Staffordshire factories was a deep blue. Today, the paint and glazing colours on Staffordshire ornaments give

The Comforter Dog

USUALLY SOLD IN PAIRS, COMFORTER DOGS – MODELLED ON A SPANIEL-LIKE BREED OF LAP DOG – WERE AMONG THE MOST POPULAR TYPES OF STAFFORDSHIRE ANIMAL.

AVAILABLE IN A VARIETY OF SIZES, THE DOGS WERE WHITE WITH COLOURED SPOTS, THEIR EARS OR NOSES PAINTED CHESTNUT, RED OR GOLD. EYES WERE ORIGINALLY MADE WITH REAL LASHES AND THE PADLOCK AND CHAIN AT THE NECK WAS PAINTED IN GILT.

THE DOGS WERE SO POPULAR THAT REPRODUCTIONS HAVE BEEN MADE ALMOST CONTINUOUSLY UP TO THE PRESENT DAY. MANY COPIES ARE SOLD AS SUCH, BUT THE UNWARY CAN EASILY MISTAKE A REPRODUCTION FIGURE FOR AN ORIGINAL.

COPIES ARE GENERALLY MADE, NOT FROM THE ORIGINAL MOULDS, BUT FROM MOULDS TAKEN FROM A GENUINE FIGURE. AS WELL AS HAVING THINNER WALLS AND BEING LIGHTER IN WEIGHT, COLOURS MAY BE FADED AND POOR.

▲ THE POPULAR DOGS APPEARED IN MANY FORMS – HERE THEY PROVIDE DECORATION FOR THIS ORNAMENTAL CLOCK.

① DISTINCTIVE OUTLINING OF EYES. MANY DOGS ALSO HAVE 'EYEBROWS'

② MOULDED LOCK AND CHAIN AT NECK, OFTEN GILT PAINTED

③ BODY EITHER WHITE OR WITH RED/ RUST/BLACK PATCHES

④ FRONT LEGS EITHER MOULDED TOGETHER OR SEPARATELY

① **FLATBACK FRONT**

② **FLATBACK REVERSE**

③ **NATURAL CRAZING**

④ **APPLIED DETAIL**

① STAFFORDSHIRE 'FLATBACK' FIGURES WERE MODELLED WITH ALL THE DETAIL ON THE FRONT OF THE ORNAMENT.

② THE REVERSE OF THE 'FLATBACK' IS ALMOST COMPLETELY FLAT AND UNPAINTED. THIS MADE ECONOMIC SENSE, AND MATTERED LITTLE WHEN FIGURES STOOD ON THE MANTEL SHELF.

③ ORIGINAL GLAZE CRAZES NATURALLY WITH TIME. DARK CRAZING WHICH IS TOO UNIFORM MAY INDICATE A FAKE — NEW GLAZES HAVE BEEN PRODUCED WHICH CRAZE ON FIRING.

④ FLOWER DECORATION APPEARS ON MANY STAFFORDSHIRE ORNAMENTS. IT WAS NOT MOULDED BUT FORMED WITH TINY FLAKES OF SOFT CLAY WHICH WERE PRESSED ON BEFORE GLAZING.

ANTIQUE OR REPRODUCTION?

TODAY STAFFORDSHIRE IS STILL PRODUCING MODELS OF THE COMFORTER DOG. ALTHOUGH ATTRACTIVE IN THEMSELVES, THE SHINY GLAZE AND REGULAR PAINTING ON THESE MODERN DOGS (ABOVE) IS VERY OBVIOUSLY NEW.

collectors some important clues to dates. The rich cobalt blue typically used for uniforms was hardly used after 1860. Look also at the colour of any gilding as this too can give an indication of age. The new liquid gilding introduced in the 1850s was much brighter in colour than the type previously used.

COPIES AND FORGERIES

Victorian Staffordshire figures and animals are fairly easy to recognize at antique markets and fairs, but because so few were marked or stamped, proving authenticity can sometimes be a problem. Many copies have been made, particularly of the popular Comforter dogs, and although not always intended to deceive, these reproductions are sometimes passed off as originals.

The most difficult reproductions to spot are those made by the Sampson Smith factory, which produced figures from original moulds unearthed after World War II.

POINTS TO WATCH

■ Look at the condition of the ornament — avoid buying damaged pieces unless they are particularly cheap or rare.

■ Examine the detail — copies cast from moulds made from original pieces will have lost much of their detail.

■ Study the painting — colours may have a rather 'flat' appearance and the features may be too neatly painted.

■ Inspect the glaze carefully, forgeries tend to have more uniform crazing than the originals as special glazes have been reproduced which craze instantly on firing.

■ Study the underside of the ornament — copies have an unglazed, wiped appearance, whereas originals are often partially glazed and show residues of kiln grit.

A pottery case for a pocket watch.

West Country Pottery

The boldly painted pottery of the West Country combined stylish design with handmade spontaneity. Each piece was individually crafted and therefore unique

Towards the end of the Victorian era and well into the 20th century, a particular form of country-made pottery caught the imagination of the buying public with its individuality and simple charm. While the major potteries of the industrial North were turning out wares with relentless uniformity, a few small potteries around the Torquay area in Devon began to flourish using traditional methods to produce a great variety of both practical and decorative wares. Of the many designs produced, most typical were the bold slip-painted flowers ranging from the stylized to the more naturalistic and also birds such as cockerels and kingfishers. Other popular lines included landscapes, sailing boats and cottages. Many pieces were inscribed with quaint sayings and mottoes, and sometimes with local place names.

A COUNTRY TRADITION

Pottery was not an entirely new industry in the West Country. Up until the late 18th century, Devon, like other areas with nearby clay, had supplied a small but steady local market with items for everyday use such as mugs, dishes, bowls and crocks. In the late 19th century, however, the industry blossomed, largely due to the efforts of two highly motivated individuals who sought to regenerate high-quality craftsmanship through hand-made goods.

The first pottery to be set up and run by this new philosophy was at Aller Vale, near Newton Abbott in Devon. It was founded in 1881 by John Phillips, a philanthropist and champion of the Arts and Crafts Movement. This and certain later potteries came to be termed 'Art' potteries because all the wares were made without the aid of mechanization, in keeping with age-old country methods. The clay was dug in the local area and all the pottery was hand thrown on a wheel. The paints and glazes were made on the premises and the pottery was decorated freehand.

Vases, jugs, pitchers, mugs and tankards, as well as various decorative ornaments were all made at Aller Vale on string driven wheels. The pottery was painted with underglaze slip designs such as stylized shells, seaweed and flowers, with lively borders painted in strong, curving strokes. In addition, there was the very popular 'motto' ware which consisted of all kinds of homely items.

Phillips died in 1897 but in 1902 Aller Vale became linked by its new owners with the nearby Watcombe pottery. The wares from the two potteries became very similar, though they did keep their separate identi-

COMPARISONS

Oriental Designs

CHARLES COLLARD, THE MOST PROMINENT DECORATOR OF THE 'ART' POTTERIES, WAS FASCINATED ALL HIS LIFE BY TURKISH DESIGNS. THE 'FOUR FLOWERS' ISNIK PATTERN OF THE 16TH CENTURY OTTOMAN EMPIRE (LEFT) WAS A GREAT FAVOURITE. ONE MODERN VERSION APPEARS IN THIS 1930s HONITON JUG.

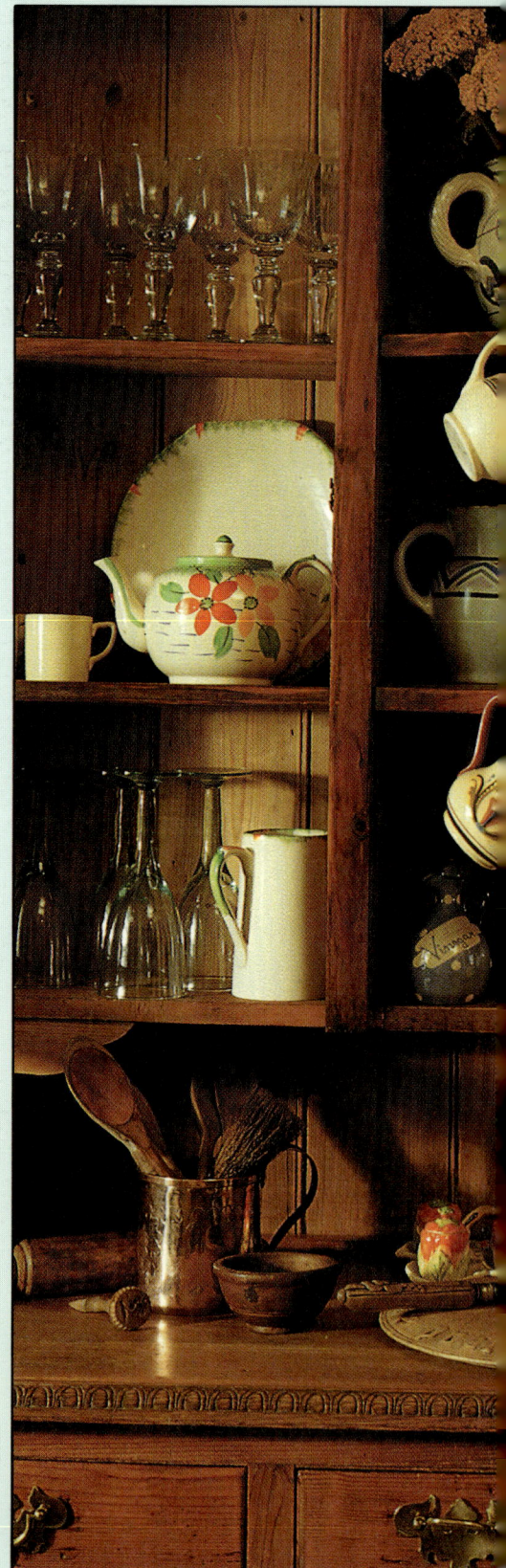

ties. In 1905, a new Art pottery was founded in Poole, Dorset, by Charles Collard, once Aller Vale's chief decorator.

CROWN DORSET ART POTTERY

While working with John Phillips, Collard had come to value the ideals of the Arts and Crafts Movement very highly. He started at Aller Vale at the age of 12 in 1886 and learnt all the various skills of a potter before specializing as a decorator. Finally Collard decided to set up on his own in Poole, naming his new workshop the Crown Dorset Pottery.

The area around Poole provided Collard with two vital ingredients for success: a good supply of coloured clay and a well-developed tourist trade. The wares produced were similar to those of Torquay but several new lines appeared, many of which

Motto Ware

THE POTTERY AT ALLER VALE, NEAR NEWTON ABBOTT, WAS THE FIRST TO MAKE MOTTO WARE. JUGS, PLATES, VASES AND ALL KINDS OF HOMELY ITEMS WERE INSCRIBED WITH LIGHT-HEARTED SAYINGS AND RHYMING MOTTOES, MANY OF WHICH EXTOLLED THE VIRTUES OF HARD WORK AND SOBER LIVING.

◀ *Strong forms and lively hand-painted designs were the hallmark of West Country pottery. A great variety of decorated wares were made by several small potteries in South Devon and Dorset from the late 19th century. In the early years of this century, the industry blossomed. As increasing numbers of visitors were drawn to the attractive seaside resorts of Torquay and Torbay, souvenir items became an important part of production.*

▼ *The 'Jacobean' pattern, started in Honiton in the mid 1920s, was one of the most successful country patterns.*

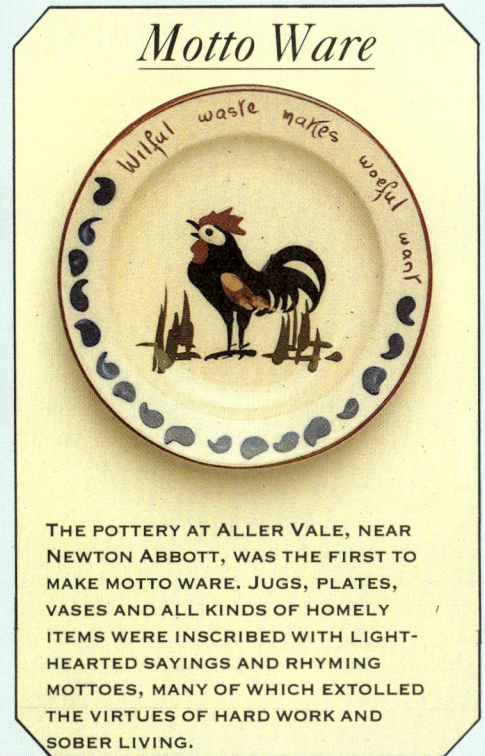

were clearly intended for seasonal visitors. By the end of the First World War, though, he was ready to embark on a new venture and bought an almost derelict pottery at Honiton in Devon.

At Honiton Collard changed his style completely. Instead of decorating under-glaze as before, decoration was now over-glaze using a new white leadless glaze which produced a matt finish, quite unlike the earlier highly glazed wares. The pottery was successful through to the Second World War, after which it was finally sold. Its new owners continued production but by more modern methods.

Aller Vale and Watcombe

The first of the Art potteries, Aller Vale marked out the way for the later successful centres, including Crown Dorset and Honiton. Aller originated a very varied range of designs and lent several of its patterns and techniques to the nearby Watcombe pottery. There were the lively, freely painted flowers on different coloured grounds. Often a coloured butterfly or dragonfly added to the decoration. More naturalistic flowers included daffodils or irises.

Eastern and Italian influences were reflected in other designs.

Collard's love of Persian and Turkish patterns resulted in curling, stylized flower motifs and borders on jugs, vases and tea services. The presence of an Italian decorator led to the introduction of such Renaissance designs as the scroll and dolphin and rarer, cherubs.

Two designs from Aller Vale came to typify West Country pottery. There was the 'scandy' pattern, and the black or coloured cockerels. These designs were transferred to Watcombe, then other potteries and, along with hand-inscribed motto ware were used for many years.

▲ Aller Vale's blue and white scroll pattern was called 'Sandringham ware' at the request of the Princess of Wales, later Queen Alexandra. She so liked the design on a visit to the pottery that she placed a special order of her own.

PRICE GUIDE ④

▲ Coloured slips were a versatile medium for design. This stork vase is thought to have been painted by Collard himself.

PRICE GUIDE ⑤

◀ Unusual miniatures from Watcombe, c. 1900, like many full-size wares of this period, were decorated with naturalistic flowers and butterflies.

PRICE GUIDE ①

PRICE GUIDE

▶ Both the shape and decoration of this Aller Vale vase betray the Eastern influence in its design. Carnations, tulips, hyacinths and roses were the four standard flowers which appeared in the 'Four Flowers' Isnik patterns from Turkey.

PRICE GUIDE ❹

▼ The timeless tulip vase, inherited from Eastern pottery, was originally designed for displaying rare flowers. This example, painted with a scroll pattern, was made c. 1900.

PRICE GUIDE ❹

▶ This jug, painted with wild roses, is typically Torquay in shape, with its handle passing through the rim.

PRICE GUIDE ❷

PRICE GUIDE

Crown Dorset Art Pottery

Although the life of the Crown Dorset Art Pottery was brief it produced a variety of wares. Early pieces use the cockerel and scandy patterns brought by Collard, the factory's founder, from Aller Vale. Soon the pottery was making typically Dorset wares.

Two unique shapes were developed — the flip-over lip, used mainly on conical vases, and the wavy top, which resembles an exaggerated scalloped edge, used on various vases, dishes and bowls.

To attract the tourist trade and compete with other West Country factories, many small pieces of motto ware, bearing quotations from William Barnes, a local Dorset dialect poet, were produced. Another range, now called Hardy ware, bore short verses specially written by the local author and poet.

As well as familiar decorative devices such as scroll, Persian and flower patterns, Dutch-style rustic and period figures were introduced. Other distinctive designs include cottages, windmills and beach scenes. The methods used for painting and firing these produced a slightly blurred, soft-focus effect. This distinctive style contrasted sharply with the clearly outlined, rather naive cottages made by Watcombe and other Torquay potteries.

Crown Dorset produced a wide range of both ornamental and functional items, including teapots, hot water jugs, candlesticks, vases, tobacco jars, jugs, basins, animals and flower pots. Mushroom-shaped pot pourri holders also became popular at this time. Not all the pottery was aimed at the cheaper end of the market. Some large, decorative items were exhibited internationally at Brussels and Turin and won gold medals.

▶ A popular novelty with tourists was to guess which way the water poured from a puzzle jug. The water travelled up the hollow handle but came out through only one of the holes in the rim. Most examples were decorated with cottages and mottoes.

PRICE GUIDE ②

▶ One of the Torquay patterns adopted by Crown Dorset in the early days was the black cockerel, shown on this beaker, c. 1905.

PRICE GUIDE ②

PRICE GUIDE

◄ *As well as the many souvenir wares, larger decorative items were also made. This attractive scrolled vase was painted by Collard.*
PRICE GUIDE **4**

▼ *A tall mushroom shape with holes at the rim typified the Dorset pot pourri vase. This example is decorated with a ring of Dutch dancers.*
PRICE GUIDE **3**

◄ *Painted landscapes with windmills frequently appeared instead of cottages on taller shapes, as seen on this conical vase with characteristic flip-over lip.*
PRICE GUIDE **3**

▼ *Beach scenes depicting a lone child looking out to sea were often accompanied by the name of the seaside town in which they were sold. The style of dress was typical of the period with smocks, sailor suits and large straw hats.*
PRICE GUIDE **3**

▲ *The 'soft focus' cottage was used on countless pottery items including the smallest of pinch pots.*
PRICE GUIDE **1**

PRICE GUIDE

COLLECTOR'S TIPS

Country pottery, with its unusual shapes and bold patterning, makes a very attractive subject for the collector, especially if interest is focused on one particular pottery or style. Many small items are still to be found at attractive prices and represent a good investment for the future. Cottage and motto ware are still relatively easily come by and remain the cheapest to buy, though it should be realized that wares of this kind remained popular for so long that they were still being made right up to the 1950s.

The larger decorative items, especially those produced by the Art potteries, have become highly sought-after in recent years.

Those whose decorators are identifiable represent particularly good finds. The quality of decoration does tend to vary, though, with the apprentice's hand being noticeably less sure than the expert's in some cases.

PATTERNS AND STYLES

The black cockerel of the Aller Vale and Longpark potteries is much collected and always makes a striking display. It appears on a whole range of domestic wares from egg cups, mugs and plates to teapots and spill vases. Some buyers favour the flower vases painted with realistic daffodils and irises. Daffodils are especially sought-after and even small items are relatively expensive – irises are even rarer. Birds such as herons and storks again fetch high prices. The Watcombe Kingfisher remains popular and is still extensively found, especially on items made during the 1920s.

For those who prefer a brighter colour range, Honiton wares represent some attractive buys. An enormous number of large jugs and vases were made during the 1920s and 1930s and some pieces are still surprisingly undervalued. Honiton is distinguished from most West Country pottery

Machine or Hand Made?

TWO HONITON JUGS OF SIMILAR STYLE – THE LESS UNIFORM SHAPES AND COLOURS ON THE RIGHT POINT TO A CRAFTMAN'S TOUCH.

The Scandy Pattern

ALLER VALE FIRST USED THE 'SCANDY' PATTERN BUT IT WAS TAKEN UP BY SEVERAL OTHER WEST COUNTRY POTTERIES AND CONTINUED TO APPEAR OVER MANY YEARS ON A WHOLE RANGE OF DOMESTIC WARES. A NUMBER OF VARIATIONS OF THE PATTERN ARE FOUND. IT IS THOUGHT TO BE AN EASTERN-INSPIRED MOTIF DEPICTING, THOUGH NOT VERY OBVIOUSLY, THE FEATHERS OF A PEACOCK.

ANOTHER VERY COMMON TYPE OF DECORATION WHICH OFTEN ACCOMPANIED THE SCANDY PATTERN WAS KNOWN AS *SGRAFFITO* — A METHOD OF SCRATCHING THROUGH THE SLIP-COVERED BASE COLOUR TO REVEAL THE DARK RED CLAY BENEATH. THE MANY EXAMPLES OF THE VERY POPULAR MOTTO WARE SHOW THIS TECHNIQUE.

THIS EIGHT-PINT TEAPOT MADE BY WATCOMBE c.1902 DISPLAYS AN ELABORATE SCANDY MOTIF. TEAPOTS OF THIS SIZE WERE GENERALLY MADE TO STAND IN CAFÉ WINDOWS AND WERE OFTEN INSCRIBED ON THE REVERSE WITH A DIALECT MOTTO.

① DARK BROWN SLIP ON HANDLE AND SPOUT, ALSO USED INSIDE

② THE BROAD DESIGNS IN COLOURED LIQUID SLIPS LEAVE RAISED SURFACE

③ SCANDY PATTERN IN SIX COLOURS — MOTTO ON REVERSE SIDE

④ CHARACTERISTIC YELLOW SLIP GROUND HIGHLIGHTED WITH BORDERS

·CLOSE UP·

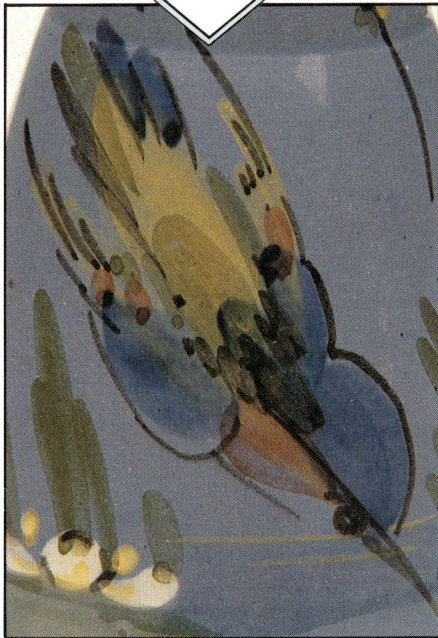

① **KINGFISHER DESIGN**

② **HIGH GLOSS GLAZE**

③ **'SOFT FOCUS' EFFECT**

④ **WOODLAND PATTERN**

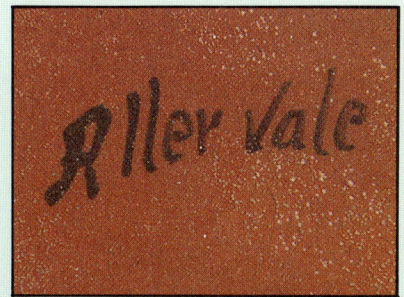

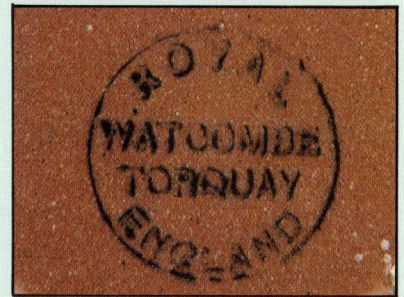

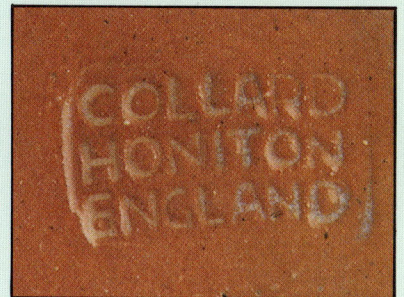

① THE DIVING KINGFISHER, PAINTED IN SLIP UNDERGLAZE WAS ONE OF THE STANDARD WATCOMBE PATTERNS, EXTENSIVELY USED IN THE 1920S

② A VERY HIGHLY GLAZED FINISH WAS TYPICAL OF ALL WEST COUNTRY POTTERY (PRIOR TO HONITON). A SHINY CLEAR GLAZE COVERED THE PAINTED DECORATION

③ THE 'SOFT FOCUS' EFFECT MAY HAVE BEEN ACCIDENTALLY DISCOVERED. AN EXTRA THICK GLAZE CAUSED SLIP COLOURS TO RUN AND BLUR ON FIRING

④ THE 'WOODLAND' PATTERN WITH ITS LEAPING DEER WAS A STANDARD HONITON PATTERN. NOTICE THE CHARACTERISTIC MATT FINISH OF THE NEUTRAL GLAZE

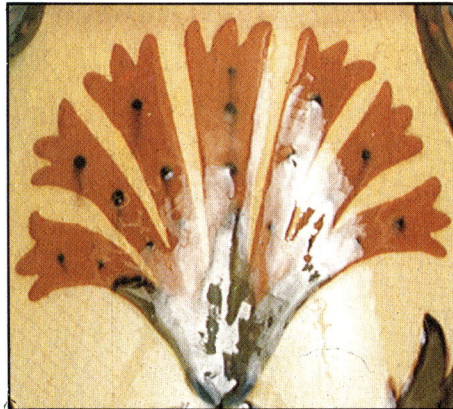

MAKERS' MARKS

MOST POTTERIES HAD STANDARD MARKS WHICH MAY BE USED AS AN AID TO DATING. MARKS MAY BE PAINTED, INCISED, STAMPED OR IMPRESSED.
TOP: PAINTED MARK C. 1900-24
CENTRE: RUBBER STAMP 1945-62
BOTTOM: IMPRESSED C. 1935-47

by its lighter, beige-coloured clay and matt finish. The Jacobean pattern, probably the single most popular design which came out of Honiton (and revived in recent years) appeared on a great range of jugs and vases, large and small, as well as on whole tea and coffee services. Also look out for a wide range of charmingly realistic pottery animals made at Honiton in the 1930s.

As craftsmen moved from one pottery to another, they took with them and continued to use the various techniques they had learnt on the way. The 'borrowing' of designs was quite common even between independent potteries in the area and has, today, made identification of some items rather difficult. Much of the pottery was unmarked so familiarity with standard patterns helps to ascertain the origin of pieces.

DESIGN DETAILS

■ Aller Vale cockerels often had the words 'Good Morning' issuing from the beak.
■ Watcombe cottages always had two storeys.
■ Watcombe birds always dived from left to right, except on 'mirror' pairs of vases.
■ The single-masted fishing boat was a favourite motif of Longpark, near Torquay.
■ The thatched cottage set between two trees originated at Longpark.
■ Early Honiton Jacobean patterns are painted in browns, rusts and golds. Later patterns use dark blues and turquoise.

▶ *The Jacobean pattern was adapted for use on many Honiton wares. This decorative plate is a rare example as it is signed by Collard.*

Art Pottery

The art potters spurned the methods of industrialization, reviving traditional techniques and the craftsman's delight in handling his materials and tools

In the second half of the 19th century, there was a growing movement to stem the tide of crude, mass-produced articles and reintroduce well-designed artefacts of every kind – the Arts and Crafts Movement. Potters were at the forefront of the movement, and the term 'art pottery' is applied to works of an individually hand-crafted – often experimental – nature that began to be produced at this time. At first, such products were something of a minority taste, but Arts and Crafts ideals quickly spread, with the result that many Edwardian houses were furnished with art pottery, which is now a richly varied field for the student and collector.

DOULTON WARES
One of the first potters to respond to the appeal for better designs was Henry Doulton, who had founded his famous

▶ *A selection of vases from three eras of art pottery. The pair on the left date from the 1890s, those in the centre from the 1870s, those on the right from the 1900s.*

Doulton Figures

Michael Michaels

GEORGE TINWORTH WAS EQUALLY AT HOME PRODUCING SERIOUS SUBJECTS, SUCH AS THIS CHARMING FIGURE OF A CELLIST, AND COMIC GROUPS OF DRUNKARDS OR GOSSIPS.

Lambeth pottery as long ago as 1815 but lived until 1873. At first it specialized in utilitarian articles, but from the 1860s it turned to products of a more decorative kind. This came about partly through Doulton's friendship with John Sparkes, head of the Lambeth School of Art, who engaged some of the most talented students to work for the pottery.

First of these was George Tinworth, later to become one of the firm's most distinguished artists. He produced bas-relief terracotta plaques on religious themes, complete with biblical text, and also large- and small-scale groups, and single figures. They ranged from elderly gossips and amiable drunkards to musical mice and even mice watching Punch and Judy shows.

A brother and two sisters – Arthur, Florence and Hannah Barlow – were among the other outstanding designers who worked at Doulton. Arthur was associated with the firm for just six years, before his early death in 1878, but during that brief period he painted extremely attractive floral designs as well as incised work.

Florence worked at Doulton from 1873 to 1909, mainly in pâte-sur-pâte, a delicate, cameo-like technique which set her small bird subjects in gentle relief against the coloured clay. Hannah was there from 1871 to 1906, producing delightful animal studies scratched into the clay and sometimes coloured in with pigment. Both sisters signed all their work.

Apart from Tinworth and the Barlows, the most notable artist at Doulton during this period was Frank A. Butler, who was much influenced by Art Nouveau from the mid-1890s.

When these artists worked with assistants, as they often did, their initials also appeared on the base of the piece, along with the potter's mark. Doulton encouraged this practice, hoping that the work would be prized for its individuality.

Walter and Edwin Martin also served their apprenticeships at Doulton's, before joining their older brother Wallace in his own pottery, which he set up in 1873. A fourth brother, Charles, managed their retail shop and dealt with all the paperwork. Their most famous wares were the grotesque 'Wally' birds and the jugs with grinning face profiles. But the brothers also produced much other well-designed and crafted pottery, such as incised and decorated vases in the Japanese style.

Following the deaths of his three brothers – Charles in 1910, Walter in 1912, and Edwin in 1914 – Wallace lost heart and closed the pottery, though he lived on in retirement until 1923.

WILLIAM DE MORGAN
Better known than these – indeed one of the most famous names in Victorian and Edwardian decorative art – was William De Morgan (1839-1917). He trained as a painter and late in life turned to writing novels with some success, but in spite of his manifold talents his career was uneven – partly because of precarious health.

De Morgan worked in various places in and near London (also in Italy) and his work shows a variety of influences transmitted into a highly personal style. Often his vases and other wares were stylishly embellished with dense patterns of flowers in the Persian manner, sometimes in a silvery lustre on a blue ground. Other De Morgan 'Persian' ware was decorated with animals, birds or fishes. Similar designs also featured on cream-coloured earthenware with a rich, ruby-red lustre.

De Morgan was keen to experiment technically as well as aesthetically. He was, for example, the first English potter to revive the antique lustre-effects of 16th and 17th century Syrian pottery, achieving the desired effect by throwing sawdust into the kiln at a precise moment during the firing.

Several of the most important art potters worked outside London. Staffordshire is the traditional home of ceramics in England, and it was at Burslem in this county that William Moorcroft opened a factory in 1913.

His designs, much influenced by Art Nouveau, became bolder and simpler after this date and he also began to experiment seriously with new glazes. Liberty's of London provided a ready outlet for his table ware and ornamental ware. Such was his influence that the Victoria and Albert Museum celebrated his centenary with a special exhibition of his work.

DELLA ROBBIA POTTERY
In Birkenhead in Cheshire, the Della Robbia Company was established in 1894 by Harold Rathbone, a painter, and Conrad Dessler, a sculptor, with the intention of producing architectural details.

Rathbone did, in fact, design plaques and wall panels, but his mercurial personality could not be so specifically harnessed and he was soon diversifying. After three years, Dressler withdrew.

The company was named after a family of 15th-century Italian sculptors and, as this suggests, there was strong Renaissance influence in Rathbone's pottery. In about 1898, indeed, he was joined by an Italian craftsman, Carlo Manzoni, who produced

Harold Rathbone designed this wall charger in 1894, the first year of his Della Robbia pottery. It is typical of Della Robbia work in its blue-green and yellow colouring, with the flowing lines of the angels and the foliage reflecting the increasing popularity of the Art-Nouveau style.

such fine works as the twin-handled 'Manzoni Vase', decorated with a painting of a Renaissance beauty set within a medallion. Other classically shaped vases decorated with stylized floral motifs were designed by Cassandia Annie Walker.

But despite the undeniable quality of such work, this highly individual pottery was forced by financial problems to close after just ten years.

It was Chinese rather than Italian pottery that influenced William Howson Taylor, who in 1898 established his Ruskin Pottery at West Smethwick, near Birmingham, to emulate this fine work. The simply shaped pottery he produced is interesting primarily for its decorative glazes.

He produced three main types of pottery: Soufflé Wares decorated in shades of a single colour; Lustre Wares in a wide range of colours and shades; and his experimental High-Fired Wares. These latter wares featured dramatic colour combinations such as purple and black streaks on a sea-green ground, and black and green on cream.

Before his death in 1935, Howson Taylor destroyed all his notes and equipment to prevent posthumous imitation of his famous glazes.

It would be wrong to suggest that the potters mentioned here, and others such as William Burton and Richard Joyce at Pilkington's, were in a majority. The mass market still demanded 'value for money' in terms of ornateness and embellishment and many potteries were only too happy to continue 'cheap-lines'. But the struggle to improve standards has borne fruit in the international acclaim accorded to such 20th-century potters as Bernard Leach.

China

Moorcroft and Della Robbia

William Moorcroft first came to public attention while Head of the Art Pottery studio at James Macintyre's Burslem pottery. There, he introduced his acclaimed Florian Ware, thrown on the wheel, then decorated with fine slip-trailing designs (a technique similar to that used in icing a cake).

Within the stylized outline of flowers and foliage thus produced, colour was added. Initially, this was limited to blues, greens and yellows, but from the 1920s he also used strikingly rich colour combinations.

Among his many other popular designs were Hazeldene (trees in a landscape), Claremont (a toadstool motif), and numerous flower and fruit designs.

In 1913 he opened his own pottery at Cobridge, becoming noted for his Chinese-type flambé glazes, and in 1930 he was appointed potter to Queen Mary.

Harold Rathbone, the somewhat eccentric founder of the Della Robbia Pottery in Birkenhead, was one of the most individual of art potters.

His early wall panels and figures in high relief were inspired by those produced by the Della Robbia family in Renaissance Italy – though his medium was coloured lead glazes rather than tin-glazed earthenware or faience.

As well as modelling and designing himself, Rathbone employed leading artists and art-school students as painters and incisers, giving free rein to their ideas in the production of clock cases, inkstands, vases, bottles and plates.

The designs, embellished with a combination of 'sgraffito' work and painting, show a strong Art-Nouveau influence and the colours are dramatically bold and striking.

▼ *This long-stemmed toadstool vase was made after Moorcroft set up his own pottery and began to develop the deeper swirling colours of his later work.*

PRICE GUIDE ❼

▼ *Moorcroft's early Florian wares were characterized by the slender elegance of their shapes and the rich blues and yellows of the flowers.*

PRICE GUIDE ❻

▼ *Yellow and green were favourite Della Robbia colours. The charming decoration on this vase was painted by Annie Walker, one of many painters recruited from local art schools.*

PRICE GUIDE ❺

PRICE GUIDE

▼ *This Della Robbia bowl was intended for growing crocuses. The bulbs were planted in holes in the top of the gourd shape and watered through the long stem.*

PRICE GUIDE **5**

▼ *Although Florian ware was usually produced in shades of blue and white, other colour combinations were used, including gold and green, as in this vase dated 1903.*

PRICE GUIDE **6**

▼ *Contemporary with the Florian style, Moorcroft also produced work for Macintyre & Co decorated with vividly-coloured naturalistic foliage – the poppy style.*

PRICE GUIDE **6**

▼ *Much of Moorcroft's early work had a Chinese influence, shown here in the blue and white colouring and the stylized cornflowers.*

PRICE GUIDE **5**

PRICE GUIDE

Martin Brothers

The success of the Martin brothers depended very much on the blending of their complementary talents.

Wallace, the modeller, had previously worked as a stone carver on the Houses of Parliament. No doubt this experience inspired his gargoyle-like 'Wally' birds, many in the form of wily owls, but others unidentifiable as any known species. The large storage jar versions had removable heads.

Other popular lines were Wallace's fish-shaped spoon-warmers with their gaping mouths, jugs with monster heads and the jugs with grinning faces modelled in relief on either side.

Edwin's talent for highly intricate incised and relief designs resulted in the more restrained and finely modelled Japanese-style wares. These he often embellished with imaginative floral designs.

Walter mixed the clays, 'threw' the large pieces and fired the pottery. Charles ran their Holborn shop and showroom.

The firm was founded in Fulham in 1873, and in 1877 moved to Southall, Middlesex, where the brothers had their own kiln capable of firing 600 items at a time.

For the first ten years or so, their wares were mainly in blues and greys, and the designs similar to those produced during their apprenticeship years at Fulham and at Doulton's.

After that, their work became completely individual. The Wally birds are the most famous examples, but there were many other strange creatures: toads, armadillos, salamanders and hedgehogs – even goblins. Edwin also created some fine fish and animal designs on plaques, plates and vases, coloured in browns, green and blues.

▼ *Edwin Martin developed his 'new style' in 1898; the elongated shape and raised twig design of this 1903 piece shows similarities with French Art-Nouveau pottery.*

PRICE GUIDE ⑦

▼ *This small salt-glazed stoneware jug was made in the early 1870s, just after the Martin brothers had set up their first workshop in Fulham making domestic wares.*

PRICE GUIDE ⑤

PRICE GUIDE

▼ Fiery dragons were a popular decorative motif. By 1899, as in this piece, they had developed flowing, abstract forms.

PRICE GUIDE **7**

▼ By the 1880s, geometric decoration had been banished to the rims and bases of vases, as in this 1889 example, which also illustrates Walter Martin's lustrous glazes.

PRICE GUIDE **7**

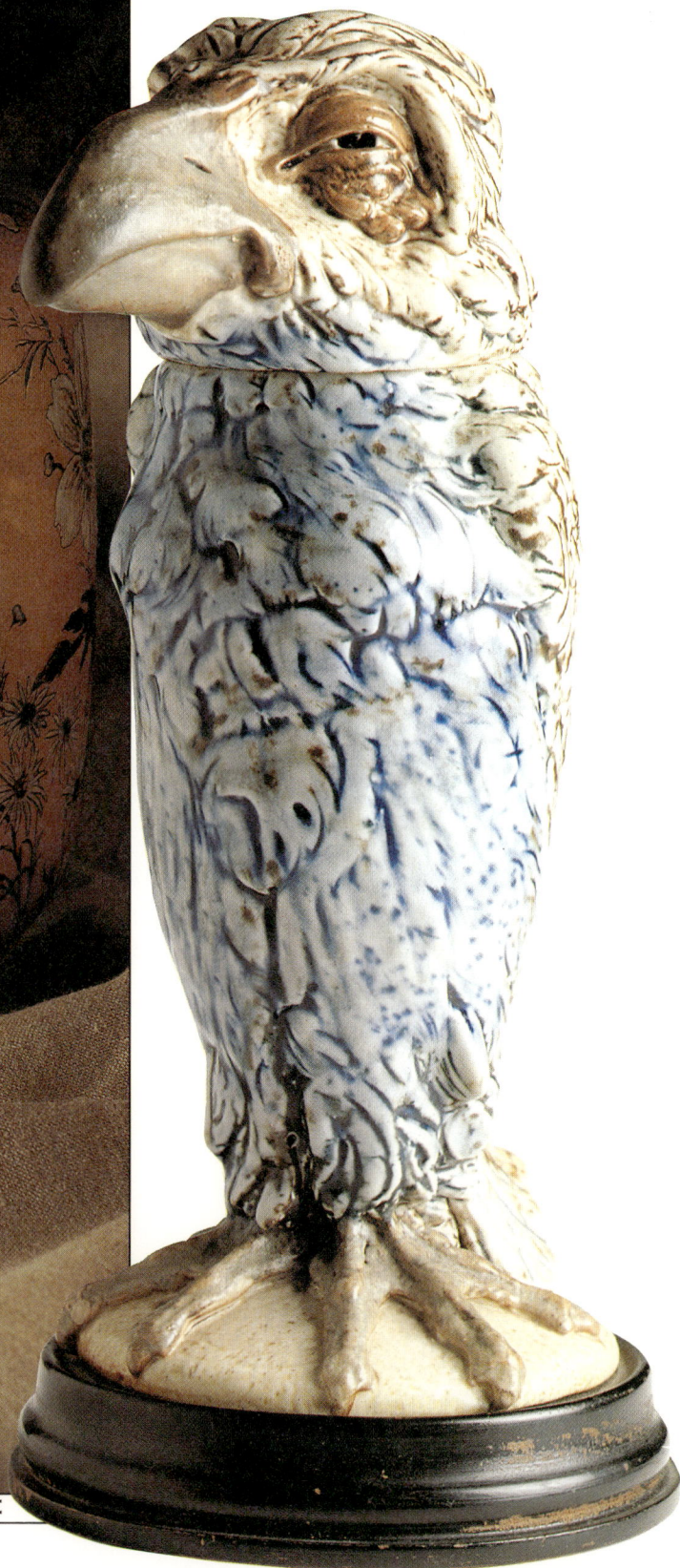

▼ Wally birds may baffle ornithologists, but they are very much sought-after by collectors of ceramics. They varied from a few inches high to several feet. This example has a detachable head, and was used as a tobacco storage jar.

PRICE GUIDE **8**

PRICE GUIDE

COLLECTOR'S TIPS

The Barlow Sisters

AN 1870S DOULTON JUG AND VASE
DECORATED BY EARLY ART POTTERS,
HANNAH AND FLORENCE BARLOW.

Art pottery was made to be collectable, and much of it is now in museums or the homes of connoisseurs, just as Henry Doulton hoped. And when outstanding pieces come to auction, they command substantial prices. However, a large number of craftsmen – and women – were involved, and their output was highly varied, so 'finds' can still be made.

DOULTON FIGURES

It will be almost impossible, for example, to find any work by the short-lived Arthur Barlow, and Della Robbia pottery can be hard to come by, as the firm was a financial failure and closed after only ten years. But it is well worth looking out for Doulton and Martin Brothers' ware.

Most art pottery pieces were not duplicated, but because the small figures George Tinworth made for Doulton's were so popular, an exception was made for these. Some of his mice and frog figures were also produced as chess pieces, and oddments sometimes turn up.

Of the Martin Brothers' wares, the later, small gourds can still be found for a reasonable sum. These can be as small as 2½-4 inches (6.5-10 cm) as they were often made to fill out the kiln when larger pieces were being fired. Despite their high quality and finish, these have not yet become popular collector's items.

If you are buying with investment in mind, rather than purely for pleasure, the item in question must be in good condition. Chips, cracks, colour slips or any other flaw will always seriously affect the value. So inspect carefully before you buy.

If the piece comes in two or more parts, check whether both are dated (as is usually the case with Wallace Martin's strange birds) and if they are so dated, check that the date on each section is identical.

This is important. At a Christie's auction in spring 1987, a particularly good owl was sold for just under £5,000; another 'uniden-tifiable' Wally bird went for the much lower sum of £1,950 – largely because the head and body sections bore different dates, suggesting they were not originally a pair.

Remember, too, that these potters had their imitators. Just one example of designs thus abused is Wallace Martin's grinning head jugs. But the copies are never as finely modelled as the originals and do not bear the authentic potter's mark.

It is well worth learning the various marks used by those potters whose work you most admire for, as well as identifying the designer, or artist, or both, these marks can also give a very good idea of when an item was made, if it is undated.

For example, William Moorcroft signed most of his decorative pieces, and slipware and plain lustre ware produced from 1914 to 1924, but after 1906 he dropped 'des' (for designer) which had previously been added after his initials or signature on the earlier pieces. Also, if you find a piece that seems almost certainly to be his, but does *not* bear his mark, reconsider carefully, as Moorcroft signed pieces only when he was completely satisfied with them.

The Martin Brothers always marked their wares with the name of the pottery, its location and usually the month and year in which it was produced. And from 1882 the signature changed from simply R. W. Martin to R. W. Martin & Brothers (or

Martin Face Jugs

IN THE 1890S, WALLACE MARTIN MADE A SERIES OF GROTESQUE FACE JUGS. SOME HAD ONE FACE, MOST TWO. MANY WERE ONE-OFFS BUT A FEW WERE CAST FROM MOULDS. ALL HAD A RICH BROWN SALT-GLAZE FINISH AND WERE MODELLED WITH REALISTIC, EXPRESSIVE FACES.

MARTIN COMBINED A DEEP RELIGIOSITY WITH A FASHIONABLE PAGAN STREAK, EXPRESSED IN THE GOLDEN SUNBURSTS OF LUXURIANT FOLIATE HAIR THAT FRAMED THE FACES. THE INCISED FLAG WAS PERHAPS A RESPONSE TO THE BOER WAR IN 1899, WHEN THIS JUG WAS MADE.

① RICH BROWN SALT GLAZE.

② FACE MODELLED TO REFLECT A LIVELY PERSONALITY.

③ PAGAN INFLUENCE IN TWINED HAIR AND FOLIAGE.

④ FLAG AS A PATRIOTIC GESTURE.

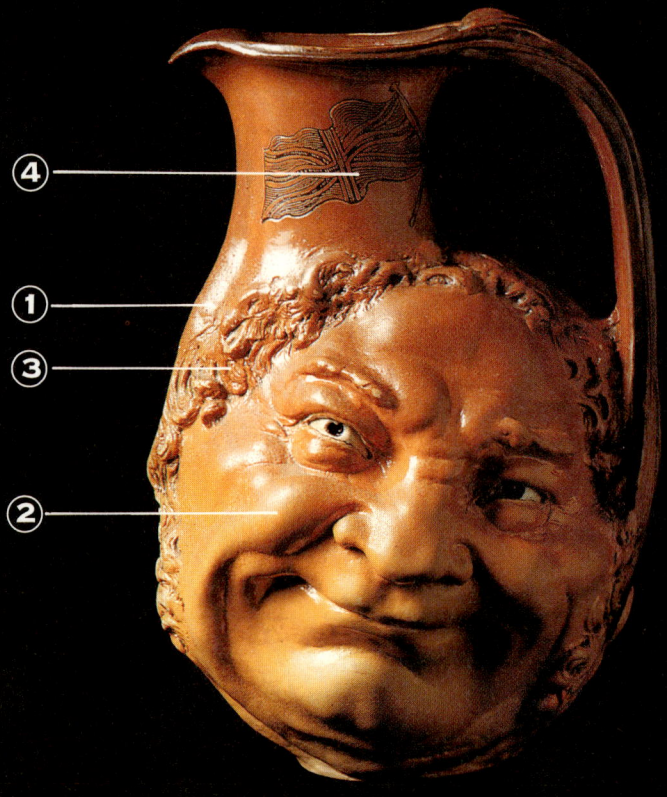

Gourd Vase

WARES IMITATING THE TEXTURES AND SHAPES OF NATURAL OBJECTS WERE MADE BY THE MARTINS IN THE 1900s.

Bros.). In all, there were five different marks.

The Doulton artists usually inscribed their initials on the base of every design. If assistants also worked on a piece, they, too, were credited. Sometimes artists or assistants worked for a company only briefly, so their names can be a very sure indication of dating. Where a particular potter or pottery was awarded Royal patronage (as with Moorcroft in 1930) this, too, will be recorded on the base.

COLOURS AND GLAZES

Because there was so much experimentation with glazes and colours during this period, these can help identify a potter or help verify a likely date.

Doulton's, for example, introduced various new bodies and styles from 1880 to 1886 – first, Impasto and Silicon in 1880, then Chine and Natural Foliage Ware – which involved impressing lace or foliage respectively into the wet clay before firing (about 1886), and Carrara Ware and Marquetrie (about 1877). Impasto, Carrara Ware and Marquetrie were not produced after 1900, whereas the remaining three continued to be used until about 1912-14.

POINTS TO WATCH

■ The animal designs of Hannah Barlow were usually bordered by intricate scroll designs. Not all of her animals were finely detailed, however; some had an informal sketch-like quality though these were just as skilfully drawn.

■ Edwin Martin's fish in water designs usually incorporated intricately detailed scrolled weeds.

■ Some of Wallace Martin's grinning face jugs have rather jolly 'sunburst' hairlines.

·CLOSE UP·

① SGRAFFITO DECORATION

② CARVED RELIEF

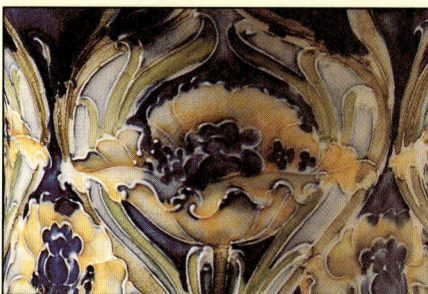

③ SLIP TRAILING

④ MOORCROFT MARK

⑤ HANNAH BARLOW MARK

⑥ DELLA ROBBIA MARK

⑦ MARTIN BROTHERS MARK

① SGRAFFITO decoration is scratched into the glaze, then filled with a contrasting pigment before firing.

② Early work by WALLACE MARTIN often uses low relief carved decoration.

③ In SLIP TRAILING, the design is outlined in a thin raised line of slip before being painted.

④ All MOORCROFT'S work has his painted signature; 'DES' was included before 1906.

⑤ This jug has factory and potter's marks as well as HANNAH BARLOW'S.

⑥ The monogram below the sailing ship is that of the potter.

⑦ '& BROTHERS' was added to WALLACE MARTIN'S signature in 1882.

Creamware and Pearlware

The attractive cream-coloured earthenware that was first developed by
Josiah Wedgwood soon found its way on to middle-class
dinner tables all over Britain

During the 18th century the growth of a huge new middle-class market transformed the British pottery industry. Demand for tableware expanded at an extraordinary rate, and the new custom of dining at a single table rather than at a collection of smaller tables encouraged the production of large, matching dinner services. Buyers wanted wares that were attractive but also strong, hard-wearing and less expensive than imported Chinese porcelain. Their needs were met by the development of creamware, a new light-coloured earthenware, that soon proved to be a great commercial success, enabling British potters to exploit the world's markets, and providing the financial support for the varied operations of Josiah Wedgwood's celebrated firm based in Burslem.

EARLY EXPERIMENTS
Early attempts to produce a durable, light-coloured ceramic body were made by various Staffordshire potters, who experimented with firing earthenware at a lower temperature than was used for such traditional products as stoneware, and then coating it with a colourless lead glaze. The saving in fuel kept down the price of the new wares, but they were not particularly hard-wearing. Then, in 1761, Josiah Wedgwood developed a new type of earthenware with a strong, near-white body and a thick, opaque, yellowish glaze. At first, the glaze scratched easily and could not withstand boiling water, making it unsuitable for the production of tea and coffee pots. But by 1764 Wedgwood had overcome all the major technical problems, and was producing creamware that was durable, pleasing and modestly priced. Over the next few years the glaze became progressively paler and more evenly applied, and Wedgwood successfully adapted mechanical means of decoration to his wares, giving patterns a characteristically smooth, neat appearance.

WEDGWOOD'S QUEENSWARE
Not surprisingly, the new creamware enjoyed an immediate and lasting popularity. This was reinforced in 1765, when Wedgwood was commissioned to supply Queen Charlotte with a 60-piece tea service; the result was so admired that he was appointed 'Potter to Her Majesty' and was allowed to call his new ware 'Queensware' (a name that the Wedgwood creamware has borne ever since). George III and

▶ *The table is about to be set with dishes, plates and comports from a late 18th-century Queensware dessert service decorated with brown and yellow vines. The blue and white pieces – a Stilton cradle, gravy boat and vase – are all pearlware.*

The Empress's Dinner Service

A SERVING DISH FROM EMPRESS CATHERINE OF RUSSIA'S 952-PIECE HAND-PAINTED DINNER SERVICE CREATED BY JOSIAH WEDGWOOD IN 1774. THE PLATES CARRY VIEWS OF ENGLAND AND A BORDER OF ACORNS AND OAK LEAVES.

Queen Charlotte were Britain's first 'middle-class' monarchs, exceptional at the time in their respectability and homely tastes, and the Queen's endorsement was of real value in promoting the fashion for creamware among the middle classes.

RUSSIAN DINNER SERVICE

Wedgwood enjoyed an even more spectacular triumph in 1774, when the far from middle-class sovereign of Russia, the Empress Catherine the Great, commissioned a 952-piece dinner service from him. Each piece was decorated with a view of England and the crest of a frog (the service was made for a palace in an area near St Petersburg known as 'The Frog Pond'). The complete service, the largest ever made, is reputed to have cost the Empress some £3,500. This sum – enormous by 18th-century standards – barely covered the cost of production; but since the service was put on show in London, attracting hordes of visitors before it was shipped to Russia, Wedgwood probably felt that such wonderful publicity fully justified the venture.

Encouraged by these successes, Wedgwood also began to use creamware for vases and other purely decorative articles made in the neo-classical style. In the late 1770s, Wedgwood began to manufacture an alternative to creamware in response to a demand for a whiter earthenware. Pearlware contained more white clay and flint than creamware, and it was fired at a higher temperature, causing it to emerge with a bluish-white body.

POPULAR PEARLWARE

Despite Wedgwood's personal reservations about his new product, it proved highly popular. It sold in huge quantities between about 1790 and 1820, and continued to be made by the firm until 1846. Many other potteries, including that of Spode, adapted the new ceramic body to their own use.

▲ *A page from a Wedgwood pattern book dated 1810, showing some of the patterns and shapes that were popular for Queensware at that date. Ornament tends to be restrained, and mainly restricted to borders, although some pieces have moulded relief decoration.*

▼ *An 18th-century creamware teapot with crabstock spout and handles made to resemble gnarled branches, and a political slogan.*

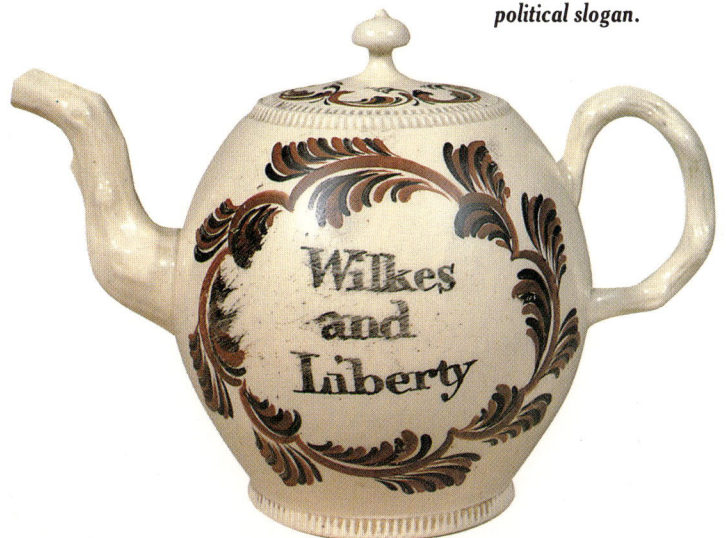

81

Creamware

As royal patronage demonstrated, creamware was considered elegant enough for the most palatial settings, but its strength, sobriety and wide availability made it particularly attractive to the middle classes.

Large quantities of cream-coloured tableware were made and sold without decoration of any kind, and in many other instances ornament was restricted to pierced rims or lattice-work, or simple floral or geometric borders.

However, the potters who made creamware catered for a variety of tastes and markets, and certain objects – notably teapots, jugs and punchbowls – often carry quite elaborate transfer-printed scenes or enamel-painted decoration: in addition to botanical illustrations and mythological scenes, the collector can expect to come across wares bearing sentimental inscriptions or commemorating political or sporting events. Moreover, although creamware is usually associated with restrained forms of ornament, there are a number of quite extravagant pieces such as plates and tureens moulded to resemble leaves, melons and other fruits and vegetables.

▼ *Wedgwood creamware diamond-shaped comport with black and yellow border decoration, dating from c.1810. The piece has been repaired.*

PRICE GUIDE ③

▶ *Creamware urn for fruit or nuts, decorated with a fret pattern and swags. The buff colour suggests a relatively early date for the piece.*

PRICE GUIDE ③

◀ *Staffordshire creamware teapot c.1770, with hand-painted decoration.*

PRICE GUIDE ⑤

▶ *Jug from c.1810, decorated with a hunting scene.*

PRICE GUIDE ⑤

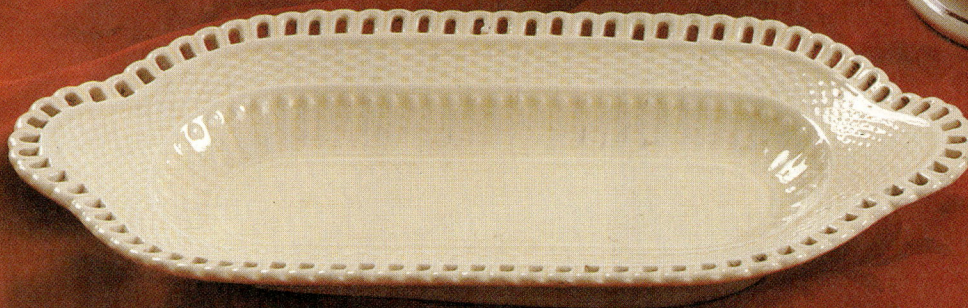

◀ *An unmarked late 18th-century elongated creamware dish, with pierced edge decoration. It was probably used for serving sweetmeats.*

PRICE GUIDE ③

PRICE GUIDE

▼ *Creamware plate dating from c.1790 with a transfer print showing a ship in full sail.*

PRICE GUIDE **5**

◄ *Wedgwood creamware square dish made in about 1810. The raised sides are adorned with a pattern of grapes and leaves.*

PRICE GUIDE **5**

▼ *A late 18th-century creamware jug, with pierced and fluted decoration.*

PRICE GUIDE **3**

▶ *Small creamware pot and lid made in the late 18th century.*

PRICE GUIDE **3**

▶ *Creamware 'veilleuse' or food warmer, c.1800, used for making infusions.*

PRICE GUIDE **3**

PRICE GUIDE

Pearlware

Pearlware is closely related to creamware, but it has a whiter body, produced by using a higher proportion of white clay and firing it at a higher temperature. Its characteristic bluish tinge derives from the use of cobalt in the glaze.

Pearlware was developed in 1779 by Josiah Wedgwood, who called it 'pearl white ware'. He claimed that having been told of customers who were 'tired of cream colour', he had devised a new ware simply to stay ahead of fashion, believing that 'the pearl white ware must be considered a change rather than an improvement'.

The anticipated decline of creamware never occurred, but pearlware, too, enjoyed great success; and within a few years, despite his seemingly low opinon of it, Josiah Wedgwood was happily making a 150-piece pearlware service for his own sister. Although its decoration was in many respects similar to that of creamware, the body was particularly suitable for transfer printing, and much blue and white pearlware was made. As with creamware, the Leeds Pottery was Wedgwood's chief rival: it made quantities of tableware, often decorated with underglaze blue printing in an oriental style.

▶ Pearlware coffee pot c.1780 decorated with delicate leafy sprigs, underglaze coloured in brown, blue, green and orange.

PRICE GUIDE 6

▲ A pâté jar in the popular Japan pattern, Imari. Dated c.1820, the decoration was underglaze coloured with added overglaze colour.

PRICE GUIDE 5

◀ A late 18th-century pearlware pot pourri and cover with hand-painted floral decoration. The piece was probably made by the Leeds Pottery.

PRICE GUIDE 5

▲ An early 19th-century pearlware goblet with bold floral decoration in underglaze blue, green and deep orange. It was probably made by Spode.

PRICE GUIDE 4

◀ A pearlware cup and cover dated c.1815, with puce transfer-printed decoration and rams' head handles.

PRICE GUIDE 5

PRICE GUIDE

▲ *A late 18th-century dinner plate with shell edge, decorated with a Chinese pagoda.*

PRICE GUIDE **4**

▲ *Quintal Staffordshire vase c. 1810 with underglaze colours in blue, orange, green and brown. This piece is valuable, even though damaged.*

PRICE GUIDE **7**

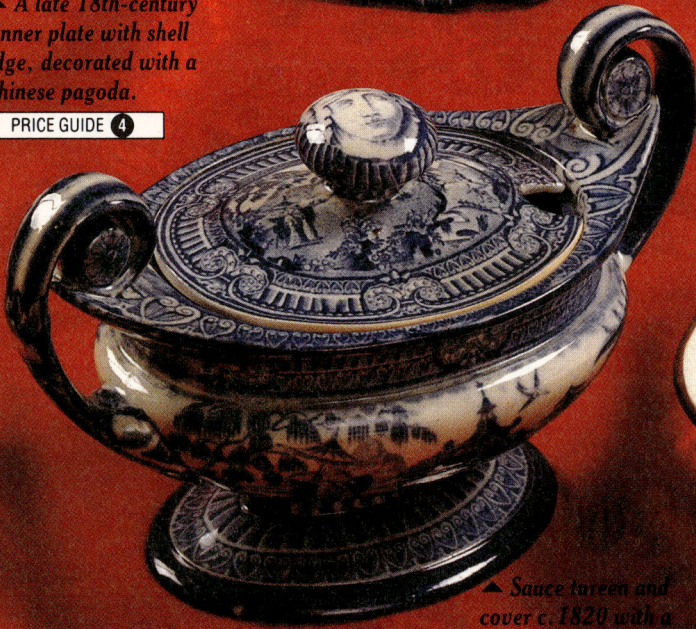

◄ *Sauce tureen and cover c. 1820 with a blue and white transfer-printed chinoiserie pattern.*

PRICE GUIDE **5**

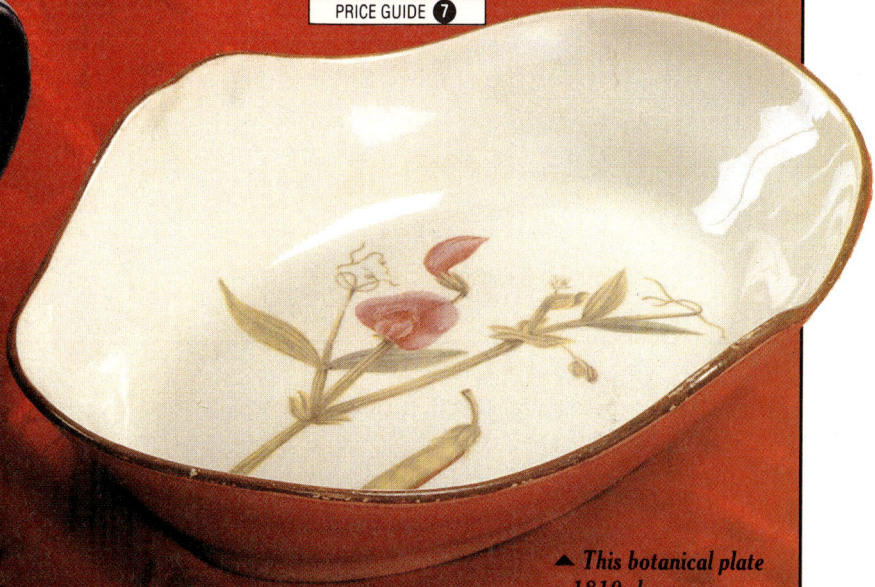

▲ *This botanical plate c. 1810 shows pearlware's characteristic iridescent appearance. The painted decoration is of a Tangier pea.*

PRICE GUIDE **6**

▲ *Miniature cup and saucer c. 1810, lightly decorated with the typical underglaze colours of brown and blue.*

PRICE GUIDE **2**

◄ *Pearlware saucer/ dish c. 1810 with underglaze colours. The bluish-white sheen was achieved by using cobalt in the glaze.*

PRICE GUIDE **3**

PRICE GUIDE

Creamware and pearlware were intended to be decorative and personal, and purely aesthetic judgements will inevitably play a prominent part when it comes to deciding whether or not to buy. Elegance of shape, crispness of line, the smoothness of the glaze and the quality of the decoration can be assessed with a little experience, but preferences concerning types of decoration or subjects are largely a matter of taste.

Authenticating the wares without professional assistance is another matter. The most prestigious are simplest to identify: Wedgwood Queensware is impressed with the single word 'Wedgwood'. Additional marks such as 'Made in England' indicate that the piece, if actually by Wedgwood, is of a much later date – after 1890. The words 'Wedgwood & Co.' were never used by Josiah's firm; they may signify that the piece was made by Ralph Wedgwood of Burslem, although the mark was also used by another firm in the 19th century. All other variations on the name, or versions of 'Queensware', indicate that the piece is not what it purports to be.

The very earliest Wedgwood creamware was seldom marked, but a knowledge of certain features will help in assessing the authenticity or likely date of a piece. A network of fine lines in the glaze – known as crazing – indicates that the piece was made before 1764, after which time the main technical defects of creamware were eliminated. Similarly, no creamware tea or coffee pot by Wedgwood can be earlier than that date, since the earliest creamware pieces could not survive contact with boiling water.

COLOUR AND TEXTURE

Another good general guide is the colour and texture of the piece: a deep yellow glaze applied unevenly points to a very early date. Although the rich creamy finish had its admirers, the majority of 18th-century customers seem to have regarded paleness as a sign of quality, which is why a good many people greeted the advent of pearlware with enthusiasm, preferring it to creamware. Wedgwood himself complained that 'it is impossible that any one colour, even though it were to come down from Heaven, should please every taste, and I cannot regularly make two cream-colours, a deep and a light shade, without having two works for that purpose'. In practice he made creamware progressively paler, completely dispensing with the early near-buff tone as early as the mid-to-late 1760s. The Leeds Pottery, which also made creamware from an early date, went through the same evolution, producing a much paler product by 1775.

Huge quantities of unmarked creamware

Creamware and Pearlware Bowls

IT IS FAIRLY EASY TO TELL CREAMWARE AND PEARLWARE APART. THE SLOP BOWL ON THE LEFT WITH A BLUISH TINGE IS PEARLWARE C. 1810; THAT ON THE RIGHT IS A CREAMWARE PIECE C. 1790.

Leeds Creamware Tureen

FROM AROUND 1765 ONWARDS, THE LEEDS POTTERY WAS PRODUCING EXCELLENT CREAMWARE OF A SIMILAR QUALITY TO JOSIAH WEDGWOOD'S QUEENSWARE. THE EARLIEST LEEDS CREAMWARE WAS A DEEP CREAM COLOUR, BUT BY 1775 – ABOUT THE TIME THIS TUREEN WAS MADE – IT WAS LIGHTER IN COLOUR.

A DELICATE AND CHARACTERISTIC FEATURE OF EARLY LEEDS WARE IS THE DOUBLE TWISTED OR ROPE HANDLE, ENDING IN A FLORAL OR LEAFY TERMINAL. MANY LEEDS PIECES ARE VERY ELABORATE, INCORPORATING INTRICATE PIERCING AND FLUTING AS PART OF THEIR DESIGN.

(1) THE BEAUTIFULLY MOULDED FLOWER FINIAL IS TYPICAL OF PIECES MADE BY THE LEEDS POTTERY.

(2) THE TWISTED HANDLES END IN FLOWERS AND LEAVES.

(3) THE PIERCED WORK IS HIGHLY SOPHISTICATED.

(4) HAND-PAINTED DECORATION CONSISTS OF GREEN GARLANDS AND SWAGS.

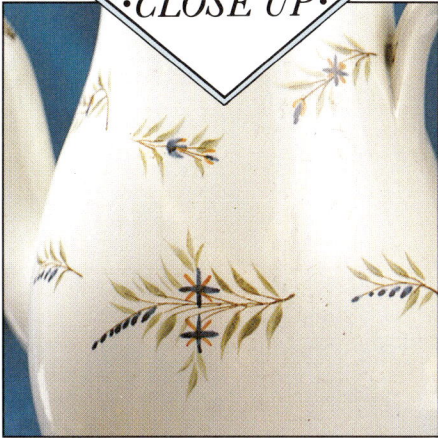
① UNEVEN GLAZE

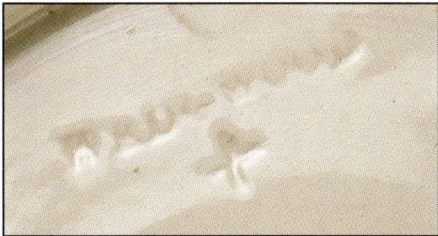
② HAND PAINTING PLUS TRANSFER

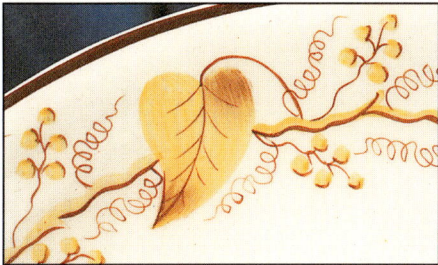
③ BOTANICAL ILLUSTRATION

④ WEDGWOOD MARK

① CLOSE INSPECTION REVEALS THAT THE BLUE GLAZE IS UNEVEN

② A BLACK TRANSFER PRINT HAS BEEN EMBELLISHED WITH HAND COLOURING

③ THIS HAND-PAINTED TANGIER PEA RESEMBLES A BOTANICAL PRINT

④ THIS SINGLE IMPRESSED WORD SHOWS THE PLATE TO BE WEDGWOOD QUEENSWARE

⑤ SOME POTTERIES – INCLUDING SWANSEA – OCCASIONALLY MARKED PIECES

⑥ THE VINE BORDER ON THE QUEENSWARE PLATE WAS PAINTED BY HAND

⑦ EVEN SMALL ITEMS LIKE THIS JUG HAVE CAREFULLY MOULDED DECORATION

⑤ SWANSEA STAMP

⑥ HAND-PAINTED BORDER

⑦ DOUBLE TWIST HANDLE AND PIERCING

and pearlware were turned out by potteries in Staffordshire, Yorkshire and elsewhere; however, it is always worth making sure that a piece really is unmarked, since the glaze sometimes ran into the impressed letters, making them almost invisible. Wedgwood's most important competitors, Leeds, Liverpool and Swansea, marked their products, but only intermittently. So in many cases it is easier to assess the age and quality of a piece than its point of origin.

LEEDS CREAMWARE

Although much Leeds creamware is virtually identical with Queensware, this pottery displays certain idiosyncrasies which can help in identification. On early wares the handles have a characteristic rope-like double twist which terminates in a leaf at the point of junction with the body. Ambitious pierced and latticed work was particularly prevalent at Leeds; and a knob in the form of a double convolvulus seems to have been unique to the pottery. Enamel painting on the ware was often executed in two colours,

brick red and black, while certain objects such as teapots were strikingly decorated with green stripes. Liverpool, on the other hand, specialized in the production of black transfer-printed wares, which were often further embellished with the addition of hand-painted motifs such as flowers.

Where it is not possible to establish the provenance of a piece, the discerning collector can only carefully check its soundness, assess its quality, and have faith in his – or her – own taste.

POINTS TO WATCH

■ Early pieces of creamware are very light in the hand.

■ Any 'Wedgwood' piece with a network of fine lines (crazing) in its glaze is either pre-1764 or, more likely, a fake.

■ Only the single impressed word 'Wedgwood' is used on wares actually made by the famous firm.

■ Wares decorated with American scenes may well have originated at the Liverpool pottery, which exported to the U.S.

▼ *Creamware was also used for purely decorative pieces. This unmarked vase with ram's-head mounts dates from c.1790.*

Commemorative China

Victorian commemorative china pays tribute to the great people and
events of the time and the best pieces are not only attractive but have
also become very collectable

A collection of commemorative ware occupied pride of place on the mantelpiece and shelves of the Victorian housekeeper's parlour. These mugs, jugs and plates, adorned with souvenir scenes of the royal coronation, the opening of railway lines and the sailings of ships, were generally admired as decorative objects, rather than actually used. Commemorative china was unashamedly popular in its appeal, and, since it was mass produced, it was affordable by the better-off servants. They bought it not only for themselves but also as gifts for others. Rather like the little Staffordshire figures that graced so many Victorian parlours, it was a patriotic, inexpensive form of ornament.

China commemoratives were part of the Victorian craze for souvenirs. Notable people, events and places were all celebrated on papier-mâché boxes, medals, biscuit tins and even bottles of beer. The idea of commemorating events and personalities in ceramic form can be traced back to 15th-century Italy, where earthenware bowls, dishes and vases were decorated with historical figures and scenes from Classical mythology. The notion was not

really taken up in Britain until two centuries later, when the first blue delftware platters and chargers were manufactured. These British pieces showed contemporary figures such as Charles I and William III and Mary. A few also showed generals and politicians of the day.

The British commemorative industry was never dominated by just one factory. Although large and well-known manufacturers such as Minton and Wedgwood produced high quality commemoratives in earthenware, stoneware and porcelain, the vast bulk of wares were made by far

Early Commemorative

THIS BLUE-DASH PORTRAIT CHARGER OF QUEEN ANNE IN HER CORONATION ROBES WAS DESIGNED AS A WALL PLAQUE. MADE OF BRISTOL DELFT-WARE, ITS NAME DERIVES FROM THE MEDIEVAL SERVANT OR 'CHARGER' WHO BROUGHT FOOD TO THE TABLE.

humbler establishments, many of whose names have long been forgotten. Commemoratives were made all over the country, but the better known centres of production were Staffordshire, Sunderland, Lowestoft, Liverpool and Bristol. Each region tended to have its own speciality: Liverpool, for example, was always well known for its china commemorating specific warships and naval heroes, while Bristol developed a curious specialization in the mid-18th century when it began to produce electioneering plates designed to promote certain West Country candidates.

COMMEMORATIVE SUBJECTS

Right from the outset, British commemorative china was used to record news and

▶ A fine Staffordshire teapot, c.1750, with tartan designs showing Bonnie Prince Charlie. The salt-glaze finish gives such china a pitted 'orange-peel' surface.

personalities in a very direct way. Because large quantities of pots or tankards could be produced in a short space of time, ephemeral events could be recorded on china within a few days of the news reaching the pottery. However, the slowness of communications in 17th- and 18th-century Britain meant that news often arrived late. Commemorative china therefore sometimes appeared months, or even years after the event. Certain subjects also proved so popular that they continued to be made for decades afterwards.

Throughout the 18th century and during the early years of the 19th century, there was a vogue for ceramics celebrating radical political causes. Particularly popular were John Wilkes and his fight against the Establishment in the 1730s and the American War of Independence in the 1770s. Other causes celebrated included the French Revolution, George IV's much-abused consort Queen Caroline – who was turned away from his coronation ceremony on the grounds that she did not have a ticket – and the 1832 Reform Bill. But the use of pottery for propagandist or satirical purposes died down during Victoria's reign, as newspapers and cartoons became the main vehicles for polemic.

VICTORIAN COMMEMORATIVES

In the 19th century, the range of subjects for commemorative ware expanded considerably. Apart from the perennially popular

◀ A glass-fronted cabinet allows an attractive commemorative collection to be displayed to full advantage, while keeping out dust and prying fingers. This case includes an octagonal plate for Victoria's Golden Jubilee in 1887 and a 1905 Doulton loving cup (top shelf).

subjects of the monarchy and royal events, it began to include celebrations of industrial achievements. New ranges of china marked the opening of Sunderland Bridge, the Iron Bridge at Coalbrookdale, and the opening of railways and canals all over the country.

Victoria's coronation in 1837 was the first time that a topical event was recorded on china before it actually occurred, as well as afterwards.

As the century progressed, popular patriotic subjects came to the fore. The heroes and battles of the Crimean War (1853-56) found their way on to endless mugs, plates and jugs. Later on, the military victories of the Boer War (1899-1902) and the annexing of the Transvaal proved popular subjects. The interest in political commemoratives died down after the turn of the century, but a few items relating to the suffragette movement and World War I were produced.

PERSONALIZED CHINA

A particularly interesting branch of commemorative pottery is that made to celebrate personal events quite unconnected with national or international affairs. Pieces can sometimes be found recording births, christenings, comings of age, marriages and wedding anniversaries, as well as testimonials to employees for long service. The best known items of this type are the large barge teapots produced in the Midlands. These teapots, which often have a miniature teapot set on the lid, are frequently decorated with floral patterns and inscribed with names and dates relating to a wedding or wedding anniversary. Chamber pots also made popular wedding presents: the bridal variety had two handles, and was invariably decorated with ribald rhymes.

Royal Commemoratives

It is a reflection of the importance that the monarchy has always played in national life that Britain produced so many souvenirs to commemorate royal events – more than anywhere else in Europe. A few pottery items were made to mark the coronations of George III and George IV, but it was Victoria's accession in 1837 that really signalled the beginnings of the royal souvenir industry. From that time on, every major occurrence in the life of the royal family was celebrated in ceramics – Victoria's marriage to Albert in 1839, the births of the Princess Royal and Prince Albert Edward, the Golden Jubilee in 1887 and the Diamond Jubilee in 1897.

Early Victorian items are generally scarcer and more valuable than later ones. An 1838 coronation mug will fetch hundreds of pounds, while those commemorating the Jubilees will be far cheaper because there are so many more still in existence.

▼ *Commemoratives of Victoria's coronation in 1838 are relatively scarce and command higher prices than later commemoratives.*

PRICE GUIDE **6**

▶ *A handsome item to adorn any mantelpiece, this gilded Staffordshire figure was made for the coronation of Edward VII in 1901.*

PRICE GUIDE **5**

▼ *This blue and white plate is unusual for commemorating the proclamation, not coronation, of Queen Victoria in 1837.*

PRICE GUIDE **6**

KING EDWARD VII

▶ *The 'clobbered' decoration on this Golden Jubilee mug was used by 19th-century fakers to make items look richer and pricier by adding enamel colours.*

PRICE GUIDE **3**

▶▶ *Few commemorative pieces were produced between Prince Albert's death and the Golden Jubilee (1887). This mug was made for Schofields of Brighton for the Diamond Jubilee.*

PRICE GUIDE **4**

PRICE GUIDE

To mark the Golden Jubilee, for instance, Doulton's manufactured 60,000 mugs to give to schoolchildren.

A number of tea services featuring the Queen and Prince Consort were manufactured in the middle of the 19th century. Few have survived complete, but it is possible to buy individual cups and saucers from many of these sets.

The royal family were also commemorated in an endless succession of Staffordshire figures. Most of Victoria's four sons and five daughters were modelled at least twice, although they are often identifiable only by the inscriptions they bear, and not their likeness.

There was no control over the quality of royal souvenirs in Victorian England, so the artistic merit of these items is very variable. The best examples come from the well known factories in Staffordshire, including Doulton Burslem, Copeland Spode and Minton.

▼ At a Golden Jubilee dinner given by the Mayor of Worcester, ladies were given red plates like this, and men blue ones.

PRICE GUIDE 4

▶ Lustre decoration as on this Edward, Prince of Wales, jug was a uniquely English embellishment.

PRICE GUIDE 5

▼ A puce transfer of Victoria and Albert on a blue background makes a pretty jug.

PRICE GUIDE 6

▶ A charming porcelain cup, saucer and plate, hand-painted on transfer, marking Victoria's death in 1901.

PRICE GUIDE 6

◀ A visit by the Prince of Wales to the Doulton factory in 1885 resulted in this saltglaze vase.

PRICE GUIDE 6

PRICE GUIDE

Politicians and Great Events

Commemorative china was produced to mark the Reform Bill of 1832 and the Chartist Movement of 1848, but most political souvenirs manufactured in Victoria's reign were celebratory rather than polemical.

Politicians themselves were always popular subjects for commemoratives, and those showing Lord John Russell, Disraeli, Gladstone and the Duke of Wellington are all fairly common.

The Crimean War (1853-56) gave rise to a large number of commemoratives showing the battles of Balaclava and Sebastopol, the notorious Charge of

▶ *Lord Nelson featured on many Victorian jugs and plates. This valuable piece, however, was made at the time of his death in 1805.*

PRICE GUIDE **7**

▼ *Wallace Gimson chose the primrose, Benjamin Disraeli's favourite flower, to decorate this plate, made in 1887.*

PRICE GUIDE **4**

▼ *The delights of J. Greaves' tea and the strike of 7,500 men in support of the nine-hour bill in 1871 are both splendidly promoted in detail on this charming plate.*

PRICE GUIDE **6**

▼ *The highlights of Sir Robert Peel's political life are illustrated on this Staffordshire plate produced at the time of his death in 1850 at the age of 62.*

PRICE GUIDE **5**

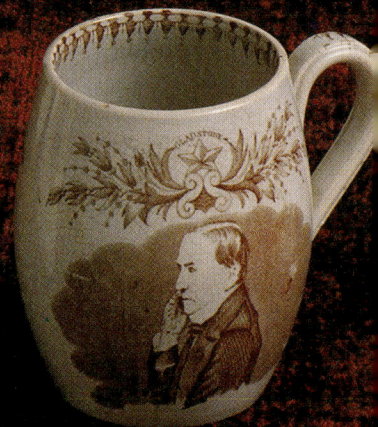

▶▶ *Politicians such as Gladstone were popular figures for commemoratives, with transfers printed on to the mug or jug.*

PRICE GUIDE **5**

◄ The Charge of the Light Brigade was one of several battles from the Crimean War frequently depicted on commemoratives.

PRICE GUIDE **6**

▼ Stanley's famous discovery of Dr Livingstone in 1871 and other British exploits in Africa recalled on this plate.

PRICE GUIDE **5**

the Light Brigade, and eminent figures associated with the campaign, including Florence Nightingale. The commonest types of Crimean commemorative are rack plates showing individual heroes and regimental plates with battles and dates.

Later in the century, the Boer War (1899-1902) provided another occasion for patriotic fervour. Popular ceramics of the time depict General Gordon and other military heroes.

The most famous civilian occasion recorded on china dur-

ing the Victorian period was the Great Exhibition, held at the newly-constructed Crystal Palace in 1851. It attracted over six and a half million visitors and spawned a vast amount of souvenir china which can be readily found today.

Britain produced large quantities of ceramic souvenirs for the American and European markets. It is not uncommon to come across commemoratives featuring Frederick the Great of Prussia or Napoleon III, as well as foreign events such as the American Civil War.

▼ A further example of a Crimean War piece from the Staffordshire potteries, showing soldiers receiving the post before the siege of Sebastopol in 1854.

PRICE GUIDE **5**

▼ Plates such as this one, made in 1900 during the Boer War, were designed to inspire the nation with patriotic feeling during the three-year campaign.

PRICE GUIDE **4**

◄◄ The Great Reform Bill, passed in 1832, is remembered on this mug showing its architects, Lord John Russell and Earl Grey.

PRICE GUIDE **5**

PRICE GUIDE

COLLECTOR'S TIPS

Because it was produced in such large quantities, there is still a great deal of commemorative ware to be found in junk shops and antique fairs. It is also relatively cheap, making it an ideal subject for a first collection. Prices are, however, beginning to rise as commemoratives become fashionable once again, and there are now a number of dealers specializing in them.

GREAT VARIETY

The range of commemorative objects includes graduated sets and single jugs, tankards, plaques, pin trays, writing accessories, vases, ornaments, punch bowls, pot lids and Staffordshire figures. Mugs are the most commonly collected. Because commemoratives enjoyed a vogue that lasted for over 200 years, and they were made by different manufacturers all over the country, they come in a variety of styles and materials. The collector can choose from soft paste porcelain from Lowestoft, creamware from Leeds and Liverpool, lustreware from Sunderland, as well as slipware, pearlware, Parian ware, earthenware and stoneware from the Potteries and elsewhere.

Some early examples are hand-painted, but the most commonly found pieces are transfer-printed in black, sepia, blue, lilac or red, with the lettering sometimes printed over the glaze. Some of the later Victorian items are multi-coloured, and were printed using one of the polychrome printing processes. A few are moulded and have inlaid enamels.

WHAT TO LOOK FOR

The most prolific producers of everyday items were Enoch Wood and Sons; Sewell and Donkin; Edge Malkin and Co; Ellis, Unwin and Mountford; Jackson and Gosling; and W. Smith and Co. Pieces made from porcelain rather than pottery tend to command higher prices, and items made by well-known manufacturers will be more expensive because they tend to be of higher quality than the average. The factories of Wedgwood, Copeland Spode, Minton and Doulton all produced commemoratives which are worth looking out for, and these are usually marked with the maker's name. However, the majority of commemoratives are unmarked and the maker is consequently unknown.

Generally speaking, the factory that made the item is of less importance to the collector than the quality of the piece and the event commemorated. Many factors influence price. Limited runs will add to the value, while pieces portraying unusual events or local occasions are also sought-after. For it to be truly desirable, the object should be as close as possible in date to the event commemorated. Mugs showing Nelson, for example, were made throughout the 19th century, long after his naval victories; contemporary examples are fairly rare.

Poor Likenesses

THE ROYAL SOUVENIR INDUSTRY WAS NOT UNDER THE CONTROL OF THE PALACE AND SOME APPALLING REPRESENTATIONS OF VICTORIA — KNOWN AS 'UGLIES' — WERE PRODUCED.

Great Exhibition Commemoratives

A PORCELAIN CUP AND SAUCER CELEBRATING THE MOST IMPORTANT AND FORMATIVE INTERNATIONAL EXHIBITION HELD IN BRITAIN IN THE 19TH CENTURY.

THE ILLUSTRATIONS DEPICT DIFFERENT VIEWS OF THE CRYSTAL PALACE, WHICH WAS BUILT TO HOUSE THE 1851 GREAT EXHIBITION, AT WHICH 'THE INDUSTRY OF ALL NATIONS' WAS ON DISPLAY. THESE PORCELAIN ARTICLES ARE PARTICULARLY ATTRACTIVELY DESIGNED AND EXECUTED, FORMING PART OF A COMPLETE TEA SERVICE.

OTHER ITEMS OF COMMEMORATIVE CHINA, SUCH AS MUGS, MAY BE RATHER CRUDER. EVENTS SUCH AS THE GREAT EXHIBITION FORM A RICH SUBJECT AREA ON WHICH TO BASE A COLLECTION.

1. GOLD RIM AND TWO CONCENTRIC CIRCLES ADD A TOUCH OF CLASS.
2. THE ILLUSTRATIONS, FROM CONTEMPORARY ENGRAVINGS, ARE TRANSFER-PRINTED.
3. AGE AND WEAR HAVE CAUSED THE TYPE TO FADE A LITTLE.

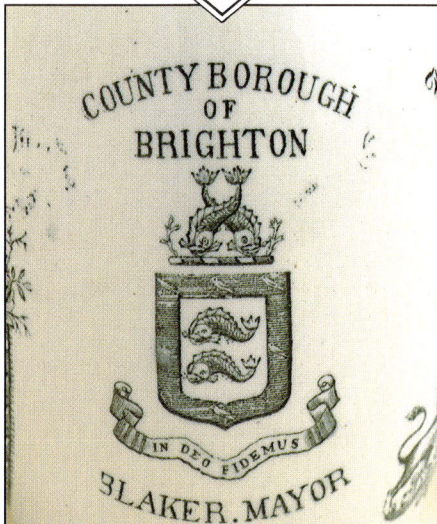

① **PERSONALIZED MUG**

② **PATRIOTIC INSCRIPTIONS**

◁ **CLOSE UP** ▷

① BOROUGH COUNCILS AND DIGNITARIES OFTEN COMMISSIONED SPECIALLY INSCRIBED CHINA.

② CHINA MARKING THE CRIMEAN AND BOER WARS WAS USUALLY INSCRIBED WITH THE NAMES OF THE PRINCIPAL GENERALS.

③ IN SUPPORT OF THE NINE-HOUR BILL, AN ENTERPRISING TEA MERCHANT PRODUCED PLATES ADVERTISING HIS PRODUCTS.

④ DESIGN REGISTRATION NUMBERS APPEAR ON CHINA PRODUCED AFTER 1883 AND USED TO DATE PIECES.

⑤ THE MAKER'S NAME HAS BEEN INCORPORATED IN A COMMEMORATIVE DESIGN.

⑥ THE FOLEY CHINA WORKS WAS OPERATED BY THE WILEMAN FAMILY, WHOSE INITIALS ARE INCORPORATED.

⑦ THIS VASE HAS AN INSCRIPTION TO COMMEMORATE A ROYAL VISIT.

③ **ADVERTISING CARTOON**

④ **DESIGN REGISTRATION NUMBER**

⑤ **MAKER'S DECORATIVE LOGO**

⑥ **MAKER'S MARK**

⑦ **PERSONAL INSCRIPTION**

FORMING A COLLECTION

Since there is such a vast array of items for the collector to choose from, it is a good idea to concentrate on one or two particular themes. Railways, naval, military, sporting, political, royal or coronation pieces — and even ballooning or holiday souvenir china — are all good subjects. Collections on single themes are also more valuable than those apparently compiled at random.

Some subjects are obviously more common than others, and it is generally the later items that are more abundant. You are more likely to find Victorian items in good condition than early delftware, and it is far easier to buy objects relating to the Golden and Diamond Jubilees of Victoria than it is to find those produced for her coronation. These more recent pieces should only be bought if they are in excellent condition.

Ceramic items can be displayed alongside commemoratives on similar subjects but in different materials. Anyone who chooses to collect objects relating to the Great Exhibition of 1851, for example, will find papier-mâché boxes, tins and glasses commemorating the same event. There is also a growing interest in commemorative pot lids, and these could look very attractive when framed and hung on the wall in groups like miniatures.

POINTS TO WATCH

■ Look to see if there is the name of a factory on the base of the piece. Modern reproductions, especially of Liverpool and Sunderland ware, are common but these are always marked.

■ Make sure that the event commemorated is a real one, backed up by historical evidence from newspapers and other sources.

■ Look at the quality of the printing. Poor or smudged examples are less valuable.

■ As with all ceramic wares, cracks, crazing and obvious repairs will make the object less desirable.

▶ *Retirement was often appropriately marked with a set of personally inscribed china. Such dinner services were used at farewell banquets, weddings or other family occasions. Today, they can form an inexpensive collection.*

War Memorabilia

During the Boer War and the two World Wars, the Staffordshire potters produced some very collectable souvenirs and commemorative ware. From the Boer War there were few heroes; generals Joffre and Foch came and went, bringing no answer to the gruelling war of attrition. Some character mugs and vases were made of war leaders – notably by Wilkinsons – but the face that appeared most often was that of Old Bill, whose transfer-printed image decorated a variety of wares made by Grimwades as well as a number of character mugs. If there were few heroes, there was certainly a villain, and caricatures of the Kaiser were as familiar as Old Bill.

Goss and other heraldic china manufacturers such as Swan and Carlton made pieces with strong naval and military associations; model tanks, shells, ships and vehicles were emblazoned with appropriate regimental badges or ship's coats of arms, as well as the less appropriate stock-in-trade crests of towns and cities.

▶ *A ceramic Marshal Foch drinks from a bottle saying 'To the devil with the Kaiser.'*

PRICE GUIDE ❻

▼ *A toby jug made by Carruthers Gould showing Admiral Beattie holding a shell.*

PRICE GUIDE ❻

▼ *A Swan crested ware tank with gold paint decoration.*

PRICE GUIDE ❸

▼ *A ceramic beaker celebrating the conclusion of hostilities in 1918. The flags of the Allies — America, Great Britain, France and Italy, surround the globe.*

PRICE GUIDE ❸

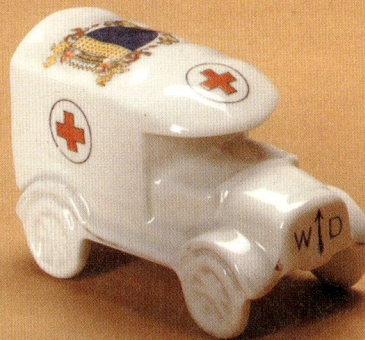

▲ *This Carlton ware First World War ambulance bears a crest and the Red Cross symbol.*

PRICE GUIDE ❺

▶ *Britannia presides over the flags of many nations on this 1919 peace treaty mug.*

PRICE GUIDE ❸

PRICE GUIDE

▼ *A Carruthers Gould mug of an unidentified general drinking from a jug proclaiming 'France for the French'. The price reflects the fact that the piece is restored.*

PRICE GUIDE ❻

▶ *An ordinary domestic bowl is enlivened by a Bairnsfather cartoon depicting with grim humour the plight of the British soldier stationed on a bombed-out farm in the middle of nowhere.*

PRICE GUIDE ❹

▼ *This Staffordshire cheese dish bearing the coats of arms of Margate, is decorated with motifs from Bruce Bairnsfather's popular wartime cartoons.*

PRICE GUIDE ❹

◀ *The two-faced Kaiser challenges the spectator to determine his destiny. Is he to be allowed to 'boss the lot' or will the old devil be defeated?*

PRICE GUIDE ❹

▶ *'Old Bill', Bairnsfather's enormously popular cartoon soldier, provided the inspiration for this patriotic toby jug.*

PRICE GUIDE ❹

▲ *Two soldiers debate the merits of their dug-out on this Bairnsfather teapot.*

PRICE GUIDE ❹

WHICH'LL
MEINSELF & GOTT
SHALL BOSS THE LOT
FOUND HIS LEVEL
A BEATEN DEVIL
WHICH'LL HE BE?
YOU SHALL DECREE.

Lustreware

Pottery with a metallic lustre finish provided a glitteringly decorative alternative to gold and silver ornaments through the Victorian and Edwardian periods

In today's harsh electric light a brown jug with a neckband of copper lustre or a Sunderland wall-plaque with a frame of pink 'splashed' lustre strike many people as cheap and tawdry, but in an Edwardian parlour lit by gas or oil lamps the same pieces would have had a quite different effect. Lustred pottery allowed the less well-off to enjoy the flickering glow of their lamps and fires reflected in their favourite household ornaments, just as the wealthy enjoyed their gilded overmantels and gleaming silverware.

Metallic lustres had been used in medieval Europe to decorate pottery. Most techniques, however, were very wasteful. These early lustres were based on copper, but the pink and copper colours of English lustreware were originally created using gold, albeit in infinitesimal quantities.

ENGLISH LUSTRE

The identity of the inventor of English lutreware is the subject of much debate. The honour is usually accorded to a certain John Hancock, simply because he claimed it. In his old age he wrote to a Staffordshire newspaper, declaring 'I was the original inventor of lustre ... I first put it into practice at Mr Spode's manufactory'.

The earliest examples of lustreware that can be dated accurately are examples from 1805 by Wedgwood, but it is clear that Spode started producing it at around the same time.

The first 'receipts' for the English lustring process were provided by a potter called Thomas Lakin in 1824. A little powdered gold was added to some aqua regia, a mix of hydrochloric and nitric acids that can dissolve gold. This solution was then combined with an oily amalgam of balsam of sulphur and turpentine and brushed on to the piece to be lustred. This medium then vaporized in the firing, leaving a thin, metallic film on the pottery.

The colour of the lustre depended both on the quality and quantity of gold used and on the colour of the pottery ground. It

Wedgwood Lustre

SOME OF THE EARLIEST PIECES OF LUSTREWARE WERE PRODUCED BY WEDGWOOD. THIS NAUTILUS-SHAPED WALL POCKET DATES FROM 1810, WHEN THE COMPANY FIRST USED THE LUSTRE TECHNIQUE.

varied from a bright gold, through copper and bronze to shades of purple and pink.

COLOURED FINISHES

For a convincing gold effect it was necessary to apply at least two coats of lustre over a reddish-brown body that had already been glazed. Purple and pink tones were obtained by including a small quantity of tin in the recipe and painting it over a white ground.

Silver lustres used similar formulae, with platinum replacing the gold. Silver could not be used, as it tarnished. Platinum, discovered only in the mid-18th century, was more expensive than gold, so it is not surprising that the rarest and most sought-after pieces of lustreware are silver lustre, especially those patterned with 'resist'.

Silver resist is like stencilling – a method that was also used on early lustre, particularly by Davenport – but instead of picking out the areas to be covered with lustre, those which were to remain lustre-free were drawn on to the pot and then carefully coated with clay mixed with honey, sugar or glycerine. The whole piece was painted with lustre, then dipped in water. The areas covered with the sticky 'resist' solution washed away to reveal the original glazed earthenware ground. In the finished article the silver lustre thus formed the background or frame for the pattern.

SILVER-RESIST DESIGNS

Resist patterns could be geometrical, but were more often leaves, flowers or birds. The fruiting vine motif, still popular today for showy dinner plates and coffee cups, was used extensively on jugs, teapots and entire tea services.

Silver resist decoration was usually employed on cream or white glazed earthenware, but more spectacular results came from coloured enamels of blue, canary yellow or rose. Early Staffordshire jugs using combinations of these colours with silver resist are extremely rare. More common are transfer-printed jugs decorated with simple bands of silver resist.

Though it continued to be popular well into the 20th century, the heyday of English lustreware was the first half of the 19th

◀ *A huge variety of ceramics were given a lustre finish, originally intended to imitate gold, silver and copper.*

▲ *The delicate shades of purple or pink lustre make it popular with collectors. Less startling than gold or silver, it blends easily into modern interiors.*

▶ *The production of lustreware continued into the 20th century. This jar by Wilton, c.1925, was crafted by A. G. Hartley-Jones at Fenton-on-Trent and is finely decorated with an orientally-inspired scene.*

century, when potters put the new glazes to every conceivable use.

Pink lustres were used to colour parts of Staffordshire figures, for the coats of Toby jugs, or for painting naive 'cottage' scenes on plates, jugs and mugs. The most common use for pink lustre glazes in the 19th century, however, was for the myriad commemorative pieces principally produced by potteries in and around Sunderland.

As the 19th century progressed, most English lustre glazes became crude and metallic. However, a number of late Victorian and Edwardian art potters, particularly William De Morgan, recreated the effects of the medieval copper lustres.

Gold and Silver Lustre

Following the example of Wedgwood, Spode and other leading Staffordshire potteries, many companies produced wares in all-over lustre, sometimes gold, but more commonly silver. Many silver lustre pieces were straight copies of traditional silverware designs, with fluted sides and beading round the base, and marketed as a cheap alternative. In fact, almost everything usually made in silver was reproduced at some time in silver lustre, from teasets, candlesticks and inkpots to salt cellars, incense-burners, knife-rests, egg-stands and even furniture stops.

This practice was abandoned by most manufacturers around 1845; if people wanted inexpensive alternatives to silver, they could buy silver plated wares.

One Staffordshire pottery that persevered with cheap silver lustreware was John Ridgway, who brought out a range of electroplated pottery in 1852. However, the platinum coating was so thin that it soon started to flake off.

Gold and silver lustre continued to be used throughout the Victorian era as decorative detail, particularly on jugs and mugs. It is frequently found on the rim, the neckband and the handle, or used as a frame for a transfer-print. Silver lustre remained the customary decoration for sporting jugs showing men shooting game birds, but it was of nothing like the quality of the magnificent silver resist pieces from the earlier years.

Copper lustre, which is found on a hard red-brown clay body was scarce until around 1823 but it was soon to be found as broad, banded patterns on mugs and jugs.

▲ Dating from 1860, this silver lustre coffee pot is Staffordshire-made. All-over silver lustre was first used to resemble sterling silver plate and was known as poor man's silver.

PRICE GUIDE **5**

▶ Staffordshire pottery conical goblet dating from the 1820s, decorated with copper lustre which had recently been introduced.

PRICE GUIDE **3**

◀ Dating from 1860, this large mug is decorated with gold lustre that is almost yellow in colour. Produced from gold oxides, gold lustre has widely varying hues, which result from the different carats of gold used.

PRICE GUIDE **3**

PRICE GUIDE

◀ *Delicately crafted copper lustre jug banded with orange with a resist pattern of leaves. Made in Staffordshire c.1850.*

PRICE GUIDE **5**

▶ *Silver lustre teapot with a delicate pattern in resist which had been used since 1810. White or cream glaze was most commonly used until the 1830s.*

PRICE GUIDE **5**

◀ *Small cup and saucer decorated with small silver lustre border and hand painted oriental-style design.*

PRICE GUIDE **3**

▲ *Small Staffordshire copper lustre bowl with mustard and blue bands. The lustre has a smooth, almost mirror-like surface which was often used to give copper lustre a consistent depth and richness of tone normally associated with gold lustre.*

PRICE GUIDE **2**

▶ *Copper lustre mug with relief moulded hand-painted flowers set on a deep blue background. This deep bronze colour was achieved by the use of more copper in the gold alloy.*

PRICE GUIDE **3**

Pink Lustre

Pink lustre is sometimes known as purple lustre because the colour was originally derived from a gold and tin powdered compound known as purple of cassius. One of its earliest uses was in Wedgwood's 'Moonlight', an exotic all-over marbled lustre. Originally it decorated anything that could be modelled in the shape of a nautilus shell, notably teacups, vases and wall-pockets, but later it was used on more conventional wares, copied by other manufacturers and repeatedly revived during the 19th century.

A more typical use of pink lustre was that associated with Sunderland, where many potteries produced commemorative wares and gifts for sailors. The most common gifts were jugs, mugs and wall-plaques decorated with a black transfer-printed scene and some amusing doggerel. The lustre which frames the text or the print is usually pink in colour and conspicuously 'splashed'. This effect was created by bubbles of oil which exploded during the firing, giving the lustre a randomly blotched appearance. The scenes printed on Sunderland lustreware are repeated again and again: the Wearmouth Bridge, the symbols of Freemasonry, an early balloon ascent, the Sailor's Farewell and the Sailor's Return, and countless sailing ships.

Many other curious novelties were produced in 'splashed' lustre, including watch-stands, rolling-pins, puzzle-jugs, frog mugs and carpet bowls. Wares similar to Sunderland pottery were also produced in nearby Newcastle, in many Staffordshire potteries, in Liverpool and Bristol, and in Swansea, where daubs of lustre, for instance, frequently decorated their popular cow-creamers.

▲ Jug with a transfer print of Queen Victoria and Prince Albert on a bright blue background which, along with canary yellow, was a favourite base colour for lustreware.

PRICE GUIDE ❻

▲ A small dish with a pink lustre border, produced c.1880. The print on the bottom is an amusing illustration of a lady and a monkey on a sofa.

PRICE GUIDE ❸

◀ Some of the most valued lustreware is purple or pink splashed, which was chiefly made in Sunderland. The effect was achieved by applying purple lustre and then spraying it with oil which produced the mottled effect during firing.

PRICE GUIDE ❺

◀ *A Staffordshire jug with pink lustre decoration produced in 1815. The border at the top has a mottled effect, as does the handle.*

PRICE GUIDE **3**

▲ *A pink resist lustre jug with a pattern popular at the time. The shade of pink achieved depends on the ratio of gold to tin, one part to four producing a light purple and one to five producing a paler rose shade.*

PRICE GUIDE **4**

▶ *A particularly delicate milk jug with small pink lustre borders at the top and bottom and a finely painted rose pattern. This was probably made c.1810 by a Staffordshire pottery.*

PRICE GUIDE **4**

PREPARE TO MEET THY GOD

▼ *Dating from c.1820, this delicate teacup has a pink lustre border around the top and a hand-painted scene of a cottage.*

PRICE GUIDE **3**

▲ *Popular with many lustreware collectors are pieces with mottoes such as this, which would have been hung on the wall.*

PRICE GUIDE **4**

▶ *Large pink lustre mug from the Staffordshire potteries, hand-painted with houses.*

PRICE GUIDE **3**

PRICE GUIDE

Collectors of lustreware face one insurmountable problem. Early pieces by manufacturers such as Wedgwood, Spode, Batkin and Bailey or Enoch Wood were sometimes marked and can be dated accordingly. The vast majority, however, including much that was produced by the same firms, was not marked and is difficult to attribute.

Unfortunately, the best clues to the age of lustreware are only revealed by wear or chipping. For example, a purplish glaze showing under a gold lustre shows the use of purple of cassius, a mixture of gold and tin oxides used only in early wares.

Silver lustreware is particularly hard to date. Designs imitating real pieces of fancy silverware point to a date before 1840, but plainer teapots and simple jugs can only be very approximately dated by the ageing of the lustre, which slowly blackens with exposure to light.

Plain copper lustre jugs can never be dated, but as they are not of enormous value, the quality of potting and attractiveness of design are better guidelines to value.

SUNDERLAND WARES

There is a tendency to attribute any piece of splashed lustreware to Sunderland because such pieces fetch a higher price. Some early pieces can be distinguished by the high quality of the potting and the decoration, but for much of the 19th century, transfer-printing and painting in the Sunderland potteries was the province of relatively unskilled workers.

More important in the valuation of Sunderland wares is the rarity of the print or the verses used to decorate the jug or plaque. Some were used thousands of times, others, for some reason or another, have survived on only a few pieces.

BUILDING A COLLECTION

One of the most satisfying finds is a jug or tankard that carries a name or a date. These are presentation pieces, given to someone to mark a special occasion. Usually made in Sunderland, they carried a standard print and set of verses, with a wreathed panel reserved for the name of the

---

COMPARISONS

Commemorative Ware

LUSTRE DECORATION HAS LONG BEEN POPULAR FOR COMMEMORATIVE WARE. THE PINK LUSTRE CUP AND SAUCER ON THE RIGHT WAS PRODUCED c.1896 TO MARK THE OPENING OF TOWER BRIDGE; THAT ON THE LEFT WAS PRODUCED BY MALING IN 1953 TO MARK THE QUEEN'S CORONATION.

Sunderland Lustre

THIS UNUSUAL SUNDERLAND LUSTRE TEAPOT DATES FROM THE LATE 19TH CENTURY, ALTHOUGH MUCH OF THE LUSTRE MADE IN THE AREA WAS PRODUCED MUCH EARLIER. EARLIER LUSTRE WAS INTENDED TO IMITATE METALS SUCH AS GOLD AND SILVER, ALTHOUGH LATER EXAMPLES SUCH AS THIS ARE OFTEN MORE SUBTLE AND HAVE LESS OBVIOUS METALLIC SHEEN. THE INTRICATE AND UNUSUAL WOODGRAIN PATTERN WAS ACHIEVED USING A COMBINATION OF TRANSFER PRINTED STIPPLING AND HAND PAINTING, WHICH PRODUCES THIS ATTRACTIVE EFFECT.

① LID FASHIONED IN PEWTER; AN UNUSUAL FEATURE ON LUSTREWARE.

② INTRICATE PATTERN WHICH LOOKS ALMOST LIKE WOOD GRAIN.

③ A DELICATE METALLIC SHEEN THAT IS SUBTLER THAN MANY LUSTRE ITEMS.

④ PARTICULARLY FINE TRANSFER-PRINTED STIPPLING AND HAND-PAINTING.

·CLOSE UP·

① MALING WARE

② RESIST LUSTRE

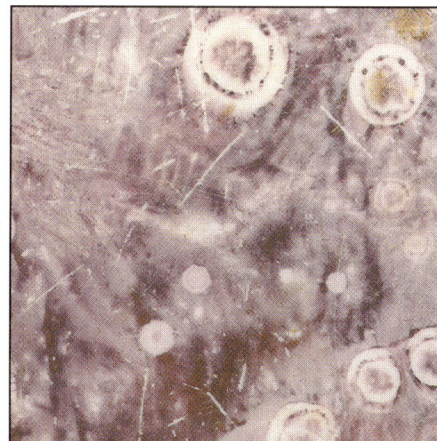

③ SPLASHED LUSTRE

④ STENCILLED LUSTRE

⑤ HAND PAINTING

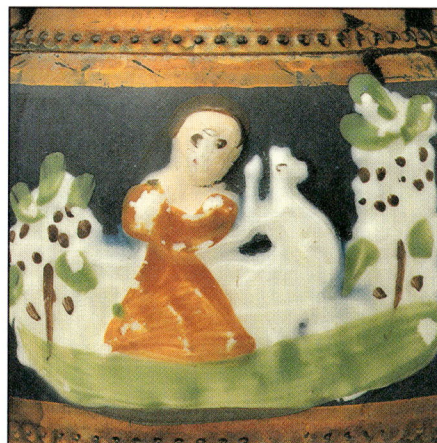

⑥ RELIEF MOULDING

① MALING PRODUCED MUCH OF THE LUSTREWARE PRODUCED IN THE 20TH CENTURY, WHEN PALER PASTEL COLOURS BECAME FASHIONABLE.

④ IN A REVERSE PROCESS OF RESIST, THE SILVER LUSTRE SEEN HERE WAS STENCILLED ON OVER THE SURFACE AND THEN DECORATED WITH PAINT.

② TO PRODUCE SILVER-RESIST LUSTREWARE, THE PATTERN WAS BLOCKED OUT WITH GLYCERINE AND THE BACKGROUND COATED WITH METAL.

⑤ A NUMBER OF PINK LUSTREWARE DESIGNS ARE DECORATED WITH HAND PAINTING, WHICH CAN BE IDENTIFIED BY ITS IRREGULAR, BOLD STROKES.

③ THIS SPLASHED-LUSTRE EFFECT WAS OFTEN USED ON PURPLE OR PINK LUSTREWARE PRODUCED IN SUNDERLAND.

⑥ RELIEF PATTERNS WERE SOMETIMES USED TO DECORATE MUGS AND VASES. THIS EXAMPLE IS RATHER CRUDELY HAND PAINTED.

recipient and the date of the presentation.

Anyone setting out to collect lustreware will soon realise that, for the sake of their display, it is wise to concentrate on one type of ware. Silver resist and stencilled silver are very rare and command the highest prices. At the other end of the scale are simple copper lustre jugs, often with some rather poor relief moulding, that are still made today.

Between these two extremes there is an enormous variety of styles, colours and manufacturers to collect. Perhaps the greatest satisfaction comes from finding something that matches a piece you already have in your collection. You might succeed in forming a pair of silver lustre candle-sticks, finding a saucer to match a cup, or even building up a set of graduated Sunderland jugs.

POINTS TO WATCH

■ Judge the piece first as a piece of pottery before considering the lustre.

■ A good, plain jug with a little lustre banding may be a better buy than a flashier piece with all-over decoration.

■ False marks are rare on lustre, but make sure no marks have been removed to make the piece seem older.

■ Be wary of very early dates ascribed to silver lustre. Early silver lustre should have become grey and dull, but this is not an infallible test.

▲ *This unusual piece of pink lustreware is actually a shaving mug. It was manufactured in the late 19th century and is rather crudely made.*

Victorian Scent Holders

In past centuries, scenting rooms was commonplace. The Victorians used china pot-pourri pots and pastille burners as sweet-smelling, decorative features in the bedroom

In the times before disinfectant, dry cleaning and efficient drains, the need to dispel foul odours and ward off disease was of paramount importance. Sweet-smelling concoctions were liberally used throughout the ages. For example, in the 7th century AD, people strewed their castle and manor floors with scented rushes and herbs. The practice of scenting rooms was carried out in different ways over the following centuries and certainly up to the Victorian period.

POMANDERS AND POT-POURRIS

By Tudor times, pomanders hung in closets and dressing rooms. These were made from oranges stuck with cloves and suspended on ribbons, or were pierced silver gilt baubles filled with lavender, nutmeg or cinnamon.

Pot-pourri, which literally translated means 'rotten pot', was an invention of the French court which swiftly wafted its way over the Channel. It became particularly popular in Elizabethan times and many recipes date from this period. The usual base was dried rose petals, to which other dried flowers and a fixitive were added. The mix was probably kept in closed pots, which were opened when necessary.

Although no Elizabethan pot-pourri pots have survived, from the mid-1700s tall, elegant pot-pourri vases and covers, sculptured in fine porcelain, were being produced at St. Cloud and Vincennes in France.

By the 1760s in England, the Derby works under William Duesbury were producing exceptionally beautiful 'frill vases', encrusted with flowers, butterflies and other decorations. The finial was usually a bird and the cover was removable. The neck and/or top sides of the case were pierced with holes to let the scent out.

FLOWER BRICKS AND BOUGH POTS

At the same time, Liverpool and Staffordshire factories were producing delft and salt-glazed flower bricks. These are so-called because of their shape – a porcelain rectangle with holes pierced in the top – and were used to hold flower heads.

Elegant bough pots took over from the flower bricks. English firms like Derby produced these bombe-shaped câche-pots, whose removable covers had several holes to hold fragrant twigs.

By the late 18th century, numerous factories were turning out ginger-jar shaped pot-pourri pots, including Chelsea-Derby, Derby, Worcester, Spode and Coalport. For the most part, they were elaborate confections, swirling with swags and garlands. Examples by Wedgwood show more restraint, with covered urns in porphory and in two-tone creamware, with classical swags.

PASTILLE BURNERS

Pastilles of sweet-smelling gums were burned in special containers as early as 1700. Whieldon, an employer and later partner of Wedgwood, probably made these burners in the shape of cottages in the 1750s, but they are rare finds today.

Better quality perfume pots or burners were produced at the beginning of the 19th century. These scent burners first made their mark in Germany and Vienna – sometimes constructed as porcelain urns, figures or perforated hollow tubes which burned bog myrtle boughs.

HEYDAY OF THE SCENTED ROOM

After 1800 more of these pieces, made to burn little cone-shaped cakes of powdered willow-wood, charcoal, benozoin, gum arabic, cinnamon and other aromatics,

appeared on the market. However, it was the Regency period that witnessed the proliferation of pastille burners, since sanitary conditions remained appalling. At the same time, pastille burners echoed the contemporary taste for things Eastern and exotic. Shapes and decoration varied enormously – urns and tazzas on pedestals, and saucers with egg-shaped covers.

The same spirit of invention affected the design of pot-pourri holders – there were double-handled, pot-bellied jars, large-handled bowls on stand, and deep baskets – all with pierced covers. Decoration ranged from the encrustations of earlier periods to painted panels.

But the heyday of the scented room is really best represented by the *cottage ornée* pastille burners. These little models of rural charm began to be made in quantity about 1820. Many of the early cottages and other architectural follies were quite large and made from heavy porcelain. At the same time, smaller, more delicate cottages in thin bone china appeared.

MASS-APPEAL
From 1800 to 1840, the majority of these pieces were made for the monied middle classes, but after this more and more pottery burners appeared. Modelling and decoration were cruder and it is obvious they were intended for a cheaper market. The attraction of the *cottage ornée* had filtered down the classes, and it was probably more as an ornament than as a functional piece that they were valued. By the 1860s, the majority had actually lost their *raison d'être* and became merely mantelpiece ornaments.

DECLINE IN NEED
After the 1860s, the need for pastille burners died down as drainage and sewage systems improved. However, they soon became sought-after as curiosities. Pot-pourri jars continued to be made well into the 20th century, both as the traditional ginger-jar or pot-bellied vases, with painted scenes, or as flat bowls in blue-and-white or other popular patterns. Some of these turn-of-the-century pieces have particularly fine painted landscapes; notable are those executed for Royal Worcester.

◀ A large, urn-shaped, pot-pourri container makes a splendid ornament on a bedroom side table or chest. Victorian ladies often displayed their pots on a mantelpiece.

▼ Pot-pourri was made from several different flowers. Dried rose petals were the most common base, to which other flowers such as dried lavender, marigold, jasmine and camomile were added. The whole mixture was fixed with orris root to make it hold its fragrance.

Pot-pourri Containers

The variety of pot-pourri containers ranged from full-bodied pots on circular rims to little round bowls with handles mounted on separate scroll-footed stands.

Coalport continued the vogue for flower encrustation developed at Derby in the 1760s. Worcester, Minton and Spode excelled in fine enamelled decoration and naturalistically painted subjects. Many of these containers had double lids: a flat, solid lid contained inside a domed perforated one, which kept the scent from dessicating; the outer lid was removed as required.

Rockingham (1826-1842) produced elegant pot-pourri cases in the classical 'Campana' or urn shape, as well as deep covered baskets and a few jars. Even Mason's Patent Ironstone produced some rare examples of pot-pourri pots from 1820 to 1825, with decoration ranging from the common Japan-peony motifs to imitation Dresden, with little sprays of flowers painted on a yellow ground, with a heavily gilded finial and double acanthus leaf handles.

From 1830 to 1920 most of the major factories produced pieces in bone china. The covered ginger-jar shape on the shallow, circular rimmed base was the market leader, but classical urns were also familiar.

As the century wore on, decoration became less heavily encrusted and more scenic, with the reserves of castles and abbeys of the early Victorian period giving way to chinoiserie and naturalistic flora in the mid- to late-19th century.

▲ A mid-Victorian pot-pourri urn, with two ornate handles, in white porcelain. The container is decorated with blue and pink floral designs and gilt edging. The lid of the pot is pierced to allow the scent out.

PRICE GUIDE ⑥

◀ A small pot-pourri bowl, complete with lid. The china is cream coloured, decorated with floral motifs. The handle of the lid is pierced to let out the pot-pourri's scent; smaller apertures mean the mixture retains its scent for longer.

PRICE GUIDE ④

PRICE GUIDE

▼ Oval, tureen-shaped pot-pourri container with pierced lid. This piece is made from creamware with brown decoration and has two handles. It is a rare example, reminiscent of caneware.

PRICE GUIDE **7**

▼ Pale mauve, ginger-jar shaped pot with gold decoration. Made of porcelain by Spode around 1830, the jar is embellished with moulded cherubs around the base. The jar is slightly chipped.

PRICE GUIDE **5**

▼ China pot-pourri jar with floral design. The container is ginger-jar shaped with two handles. The outer lid lifts off to reveal an inner lid with pierced holes, and was removed when required.

PRICE GUIDE **5**

▲ Staffordshire pot-pourri container in an upright, vase shape. In this early 19th century example, the grey china is decorated with blue moulding and has been attractively finished with a gilt edge.

PRICE GUIDE **5**

PRICE GUIDE

Pastille Burners

Many pastille burners from the early 19th century followed the same pattern as pot-pourri containers, often taking the form of small, Grecian-style covered vases. Worcester and Derby produced elegant bone china incense burners with removable pierced lids in this form.

Spode, Derby and Davenport all sold a conical version which fitted like a snuffer onto a square base mounted on ball feet. The cover was painted with flowers or fruit, and the finial was a hollow gilded frame which siphoned the scented smoke around the room.

The fashion for *cottage ornée* pastille burners lasted from 1820 to 1860, and these are highly collectable today. The term covers a wide field, since not all the pieces were cottages – although the thatched and timbered Tudor cottages were among the most popular of the subjects.

Other designs included turretted castles and gateways, clock towers, toll-houses, lighthouses, Chinese pagodas, Gothic follies and sometimes churches. The majority were rectangular in design, but circular, hexagonal and irregular shapes also occurred.

The Staffordshire potteries covered their creations in naturalistic encrustations. Flowers were often moulded in full relief, the grass and roof moss given rough texture by a coarse shaving of paste, and tiles and bricks picked out in gilt.

As the century wore on, the modelling became less expert and the gilding and colouring more slap-dash, although the better-known factories continued to produce some attractive pieces.

▶ *A Staffordshire clock tower with turrets, dating from 1870. The white pottery is decorated with colourful flower encrustations and gold paint.*

PRICE GUIDE **5**

▶ *Staffordshire cottage in a grander style. This three-tiered model is decorated with flowers, and is a rather curious fantasy of the rustic style.*

PRICE GUIDE **5**

▶ *Thatched cottage ornée dating from 1860. The style of the cottage depended on the room it was intended for and the market. Plainer, rustic examples were displayed in more informal rooms.*

PRICE GUIDE **5**

◀ *Late 19th century cottage. The gabled roof has been attractively embellished, and the windows are complementary in shape. The cottage is decorated with floral additions, and a tree or hillock looms over the roof.*

PRICE GUIDE **5**

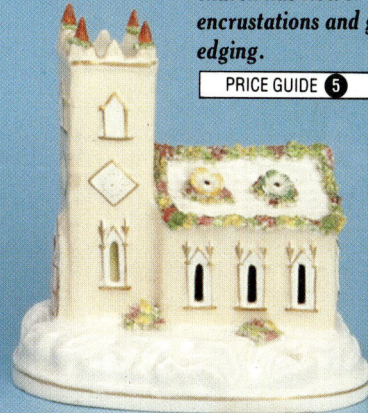

▼ *Church cottage ornée with clock tower. Made of porcelain, this model church has flower encrustations and gilt edging.*

PRICE GUIDE **5**

◀ *A Staffordshire castle with turrets, dating from 1870. Each door has a crucifix above. The gold paint has rubbed away from the edge of the rust-coloured doors.*

PRICE GUIDE **5**

▼ *This mushroom-shaped porcelain cottage is a fine example of rustic fantasy design. The circular roof and base of the cottage are dotted with out-sized flowers.*

PRICE GUIDE **4**

◀ *This cottage ornée is designed in the Gothic style, with long, slender windows and towers flanking either side. Typically, the flowers are larger than life size.*

PRICE GUIDE **5**

◀ *A water mill, such as this Staffordshire example, was a popular subject for the cottage ornée. The lattice windows belong to the cottage side, whereas the mill windows are left unfilled for the incense to escape.*

PRICE GUIDE **5**

PRICE GUIDE

Ornamental Cottages

COTTAGE WARE WAS EXTREMELY POPULAR DURING THE 19TH CENTURY. AS THE NEED FOR INCENSE BURNERS DECLINED, SO COTTAGES WERE PRODUCED PURELY FOR ORNAMENT. THESE ARE IDENTIFIED BY THE ABSENCE OF APERTURES AT THE BACK FOR THE PASTILLE, OR AT THE FRONT FOR RELEASING THE INCENSE.

Pot-pourri containers and pastille burners are popular collector's items today as they make decorative ornaments en masse. Both types of pieces can be found at specialist dealers, but usually in separate collections because of their quite different market appeal.

Both repay careful searching and scrutiny because collectability – particularly of the little porcelain and pottery models of houses and other dwellings – has aggravated scarcity, pushed up prices and inspired some not very scrupulous modern copies.

The most common form for 19th century pot-pourri is the vase or ginger-jar shape with the pierced lid. Jars from the early- to mid-19th century can sometimes be found with both lids intact, but after that time the double lid was usually done away with.

Like 19th and early-20th century garniture sets and decorative wares, pot-pourri pots were often expensive pieces from major factories, and today they generally command higher prices than the pastille burners.

PASTILLE BURNER DESIGNS

The *cottage ornée* or decorated building is the most sought-after of the pastille burners. These can be readily differentiated from the other model buildings of the time, such as money boxes and chimney ornaments, by their utilitarian construction.

The most usual style is the cottage or building in which the walls and roof were fired as one piece and lift off the base. The pastille was placed on this base, lit and the lid lowered over it. Smoke escaped through the chimney and windows. From 1840 to 1860, pieces often have filled-in windows so

Church Pastille Burner

THE STAFFORDSHIRE POTTERIES PRODUCED A NUMBER OF COTTAGES IN VARIOUS STYLES DURING THE 19TH CENTURY. THE MODEL CHURCH, ALONGSIDE WATERMILLS, CASTLES, CLOCK TOWERS AND PAGODAS, WERE POPULAR ALTERNATIVES TO THE MORE WIDELY MADE RUSTIC COTTAGES.

AS WITH THE MAJORITY OF *COTTAGES ORNÉES*, THIS PORCELAIN CHURCH IS UNMARKED. EARLIER EXAMPLES HAVE OPEN WINDOWS AS WELL AS TOWER TURRETS, WHEREAS THE WINDOWS ON LATER EXAMPLES ARE FILLED IN AND ONLY THE TOWER IS OPEN. ON THIS EXAMPLE, THE PASTILLE IS INSERTED AT THE BACK. OTHER MODELS HAVE LIFT-OFF WALLS AND ROOF, OR SOMETIMES JUST THE ROOF LIFTS OFF. AN UNUSUAL FEATURE IS A DRAWER AT THE BACK FOR STORING PASTILLES.

① INCENSE IS RELEASED THROUGH THE CHURCH TOWER.

② LARGER-THAN-LIFE FLOWER ENCRUSTATIONS ARE A POPULAR *COTTAGE ORNÉE* EMBELLISHMENT.

③ WINDOWS, AS WELL AS THE TOWER, ARE LEFT OPEN TO RELEASE THE FRAGRANT INCENSE.

④ THE BASE OF THE PASTILLE BURNER, WINDOWS, CLOCK, DOOR AND TOWER ARE PICKED OUT IN GOLD.

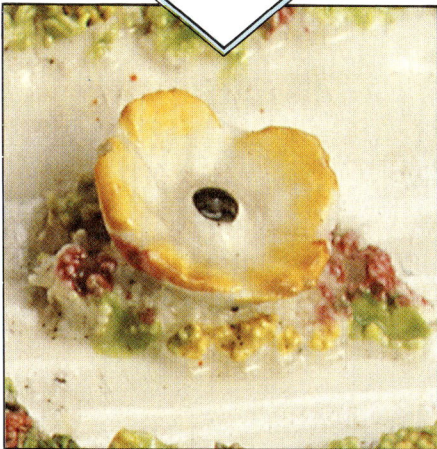

·CLOSE UP·

① FLOWER ENCRUSTATION

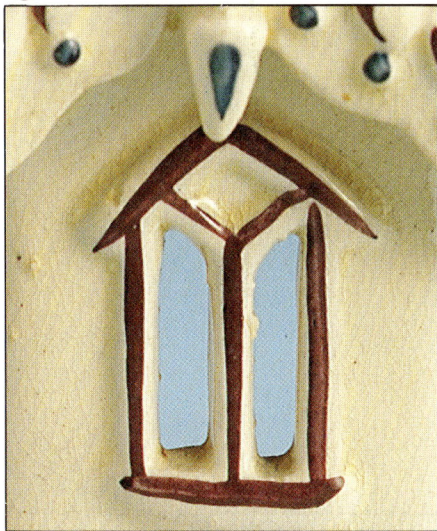

③ APERTURE FOR INCENSE

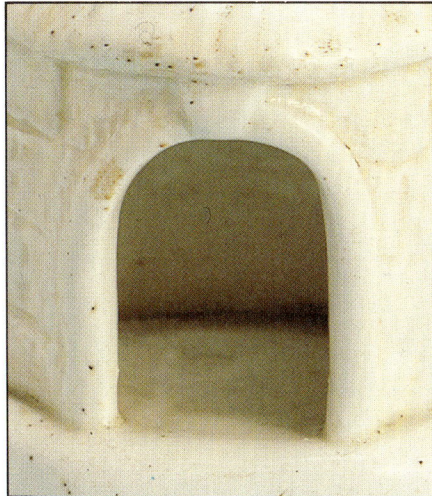

② APERTURE FOR PASTILLE

① DELICATELY MOULDED AND PAINTED FLOWERS WERE A POPULAR DECORATIVE FINISH ON COTTAGES. IN EARLY EXAMPLES, THESE WERE A USEFUL COVER FOR FIRING CRACKS IN THE CHINA. THE AMOUNT OF ENCRUSTATION OFTEN IDENTIFIES THE MAKER.

② THE OPENING AT THE BACK OF A *COTTAGE ORNÉE* IS THE PLACE WHERE THE PASTILLE IS INSERTED AND LIT. COTTAGES WITHOUT THESE APERTURES ARE NOT AUTHENTIC PASTILLE BURNERS.

③ VARIOUS APERTURES ARE POSITIONED AT DISCREET PLACES ON THE COTTAGES, ALLOWING THE INCENSE TO CIRCULATE. TYPICAL PLACES ARE WINDOWS, CHIMNEYS AND TOWER TURRETS.

POT-POURRI LIDS

LIDS ARE DIFFERENTLY PIERCED, DEPENDING ON THE DESIGN OF THE POT-POURRI CONTAINER. LARGE, SYMMETRICAL APERTURES MAY APPEAR ON LARGE POTS, WHEREAS A SERIES OF TINY HOLES OR COMBINATION OF LARGE AND SMALL ARE SUITED TO SMALLER DESIGNS.

that the chimney is the only exit for smoke. Some later examples do not come apart at all and the pastille is inserted through the door. The rarest design is where a drawer pulls out from the back or side.

Before 1840, most attractive pastille burners were made of porcelain; later examples are pottery. Original pieces have an unglazed bottom rim which fits onto the base and prevents the top from slipping off and breaking.

PASTILLE BURNER PRODUCERS

The best period for *cottage ornée* pieces is from 1815 to 1835, but fine later pieces can be found. Some 20 to 30 Staffordshire potteries made these rustic fancies, most of them small firms, with Minton and Spode among the larger.

Coalport cottages particularly were lavishly endowed, with carnations, buttercups and sweetpeas. The earliest of these cottages have 'C' or 'C Dale' on their underside; after 1830, like most pastille burners, they

were manufactured with unmarked bases.

Early Worcester pieces, on the other hand, were noteworthy for their heaviness and naivety; the walls sloped upwards and outwards. After 1830 other buildings, particularly castles, began to make an appearance.

REAL OR FAKE?

■ Marks contemporary with the piece should be found under the glaze, not over it or on a rubbed patch.

■ Beware cheap modern reproductions with early marks fired on. The crudeness of the modelling and material are giveaways.

■ Check church pastille burners carefully. These are among the rarest of original designs and many copies have been made over the years. Lilac-coloured cottages are also much reproduced.

▶ *This pagoda-style* cottage ornée *has been adapted to modern usage. A light bulb replaces the pastille inside, making a lamp.*

Fairings

Pride of place on the maid's mantelpiece was often given to a colourful
figure ornament known as a fairing – a treasured memento of a rare day
out at the local fair

Although anything obtained at, or specially made for, a fair may be called a fairing, in collectors' terms the name is applied exclusively to a type of porcelain ornament. Fairings are small, often brightly-coloured, figure-groups – or occasionally single figures – usually with humorous or whimsical captions inscribed on their bases.

COLOURFUL TRIFLES
Also known as bed pieces – from the scene of several of the vignettes – or as cottage mantelshelf china, fairings had their heyday in the period 1860-1900. Most were purely decorative, but others functioned as match strikers, spill containers or watch holders. As a variation, smaller versions of the comic scenes formed lids to china trinket boxes.

Fairings were cheap and cheerful and very much a working-class taste, reflecting the broad humour associated with the music hall. They made a colourful decoration for many small cottages or the servants' quarters in grander houses, souvenirs of happy times spent at the fair.

The great fairs of the Middle Ages were the only place where people outside the few great cities could buy such everyday items as clothing or pots and pans. In the absence of well-developed roads, village shops were confined to selling local produce.

The commercial importance of fairs was in decline throughout Victoria's reign under the influence of the railways and better road systems, but they remained great social and festive occasions. The local fair was an annual holiday – often the only holiday – for the whole community.

COMPARISONS

Rare Fairings

TITLED 'ON THE RINK', THIS GERMAN FAIRING DATES FROM THE 1880S AND IS VERY RARE. THE MODEL IS UNNUMBERED AND THE CAPTION IS WRITTEN ON THE BACK OF THE BASE, BEHIND THE ROLLER SKATES.

The heyday of fairings coincided with the last days of the great medieval fairs. Not only had the railways enabled goods to travel the length and breadth of the country, they had also altered the holiday patterns of the working classes. Just as the annual trip to the fair was superseded as a holiday highlight by excursions to the seaside, so

▶ *China fairings were originally sold or given as prizes at fairs; in late-Victorian times, however, they were primarily sold in shops.*

▼ *These popular 19th-century fairground mementoes with their humorous captions are now highly collectable.*

other souvenirs, such as heraldic china, replaced fairings. Late in the century, fairings were mostly sold in shops.

SAUCY HUMOUR

Costing just a few pence when new, or maybe won as a prize at a fairground booth, fairings are today highly prized by collectors. Three-dimensional versions of the Edwardian saucy postcard, their bright colours, crude, but vivacious modelling and typically British humour give them an irresistible, folksy charm.

All of the stock figures of fun are represented; maidens innocent and not-so-innocent, outraged fathers, hapless swains, nervous newly-weds, henpecked or erring husbands, tottering drunks and ancient lechers. Many feature flirtations, glimpses of ankles or stolen kisses. That perennial seaside command, Kiss Me Quick, is the caption on more than one fairing.

GERMAN ORIGINS

Fairings seem so quintessentially British that it comes as something of a shock to find that almost all of them – and certainly all the best ones – were made in Germany. German potteries were technically well-advanced, and able to produce brightly-coloured and gilded work relatively cheaply.

The first, and most prolific, producer of fairings was the firm of Conta & Boehme, of Pössneck, otherwise known for their bisque dolls' heads. They began to produce captioned fairings around 1860, from ideas sent to them by their British agents.

At first the subject matter was largely courtship and marriage, with occasional incidents from everyday life – a visit to the dentist, taking tea or travelling in carriages.

A few showed war scenes. Some box-lids refer to the Crimea, and there are also pieces concerning the Franco-Prussian war of 1870. Though made by Conta & Boehme, and in the style of fairings, these were not jokey pieces. Others featured crude portraits of famous personalities.

Later, as fairgrounds continued to decline and Conta & Boehme sought a new, more respectable market in shops, so the emphasis changed. Their later fairings typically feature cherubic children, or winsome cats and dogs either behaving as adults or simply being winningly lovable. The humorous was soon abandoned in favour of the sentimental.

MAKING FAIRINGS

All Conta & Boehme's fairings were solid, and moulded in white soft-paste porcelain. Several moulds were used for each fairing. The pieces were then assembled by one particular craftsman, who also added any detail too fine for moulding. The assembled fairings were given a high temperature firing, a liquid glaze and then a second firing before being hand-painted, gilded and finished at a lower temperature.

DECLINE IN QUALITY

Conta & Boehme did not have the market to themselves for very long. By the 1880s, three or four other German factories had begun to make competitive versions of a decidedly lower quality, often hollow and moulded in one piece. Some themes and captions were directly lifted from Conta & Boehme models. New captions tended to the lavatorial, rather than the bawdy, or made naked appeals to sentiment.

These inferior pieces from Germany – and one or two that have been found with a 'Made in Japan' stamp – dominated a declining market in the Edwardian period, until World War I ended the trade.

Figure Groups

All fairing figure groups were small, with bases no more than 5 inches (13cms) long. Some were made in two sizes.

Most figure groups had captions, almost always in English. One or two examples with French or German captions have been found, but on the whole the humour did not translate very well.

Puns were a particular favourite; a woman rifling the pockets of her sleeping husband's trousers is captioned 'Robbing the mail', and a pair of drunks in the stocks 'Babes in the wood'. Slapstick is also popular; 'The last in bed to put out the light' features a married couple crashing heads as they leap into bed.

Domestic situation comedy is typified by popular pieces like 'Returning home at one o'clock in the morning', where the wife is punishing her miscreant husband with a slipper, or 'Twelve months after marriage', with a gloomy husband nursing the baby while his wife sleeps on.

Perhaps the most characteris-tic style was slightly risqué. Several versions exist of 'The landlord in love', with an elderly man spying on a disrobing woman, while 'Two different views' featured a young woman sitting between two standing men, one looking into the distance through a telescope while the other peers over the girl's shoulder and down her cleavage.

▲ *This very rare fairing shows the figure of a widow in mourning. Poignantly entitled 'To Let', it dates from 1860-70.*

PRICE GUIDE **5**

◀ *Entitled 'Going to the ball', this fairing dates from 1870. It shows a young girl being dressed by her mother to go to a party.*

PRICE GUIDE **4**

▼ *First made by Conta & Boehme, this design was copied by many other German factories. The original model is now very rare.*

PRICE GUIDE **3**

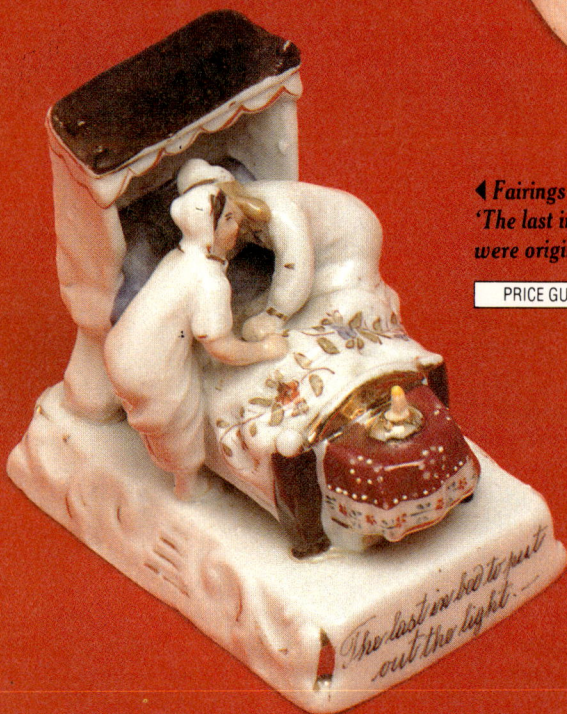

◀ *Fairings with the popular motto 'The last in bed to put out the light', were originally made in 1860.*

PRICE GUIDE **3**

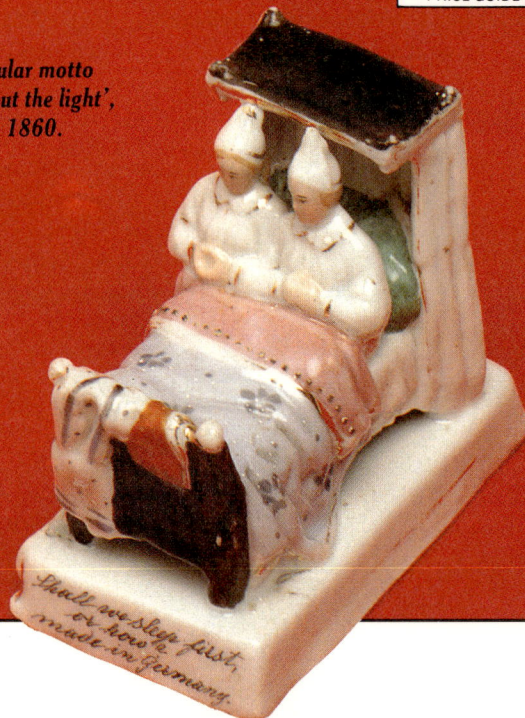

◀ *Dating from between 1863-75, this fairing which shows a monk kissing a young girl, is wittily entitled 'Animated spirits'.*

PRICE GUIDE **5**

◀ *'If you please Sir', a very rare model, shows a buxom maid, standing next to a man at a table, pointing out a cork in her cleavage!*

PRICE GUIDE **5**

▼ *A Conta & Boehme unnumbered model of an old lady sitting at a table with a young man standing beside her, reading 'If youth knew'.*

PRICE GUIDE **5**

▶ *This typically coarse model entitled 'Come along, these flowers don't smell too good', shows a couple by a rose bush with a young boy squatting behind it.*

PRICE GUIDE **5**

◀ *A very rare fairing probably made c. 1880, showing a young girl embracing her loved one and entitled 'Just as it should be'.*

PRICE GUIDE **5**

▶ *'The power of love', a humorous fairing which shows a wife peeping behind a screen as her husband kisses the maid.*

PRICE GUIDE **4**

PRICE GUIDE

Boxes and Match Holders

Although most fairings were simply made to be enjoyed, others had more practical applications. Trinket boxes had lids which echoed the most popular fairing themes, like 'The last in bed to put out the light', but with no captions.

Some were in the same style as fairings but had original subjects; a figure of Garibaldi appears on one, while another is in the shape of a barrel, astride which sits Champagne Charlie in the form of George Leybourne, who popularized the song.

Several of Conta & Boehme's captioned fairings were match-holders. These were intended for phosphorus matches, invented around 1830, which were unstable and best kept in a fireproof box, either ceramic, metal or glass. The match-holder fairings had a rough-textured section for striking the matches.

The holders were integrated into the overall design by disguising them as a piece of masonry, a capstan, a tree stump, a broken column, or something of similar shape.

▶ A match striker c. 1880, with blue-painted decoration, showing a young boy crying over a spilt basket of eggs.

PRICE GUIDE ❸

▲ An unusual spill holder called 'Welsh costume', showing three Welsh ladies at a tea party; it dates from the 1890s.

PRICE GUIDE ❸

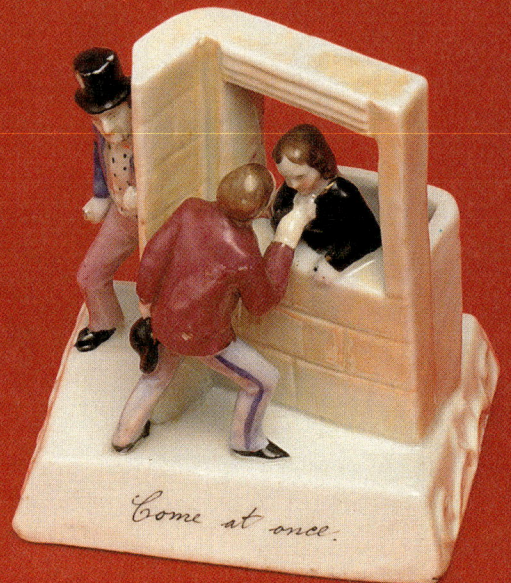

▲ A rare match holder called 'Come at once' showing a man talking to his sweetheart while her father approaches with a stick.

PRICE GUIDE ❹

▶ A reasonably common match holder dating from 1862-1870 showing a girl at an oyster stand and entitled 'Oysters, Sir'.

PRICE GUIDE ❹

PRICE GUIDE

◀ *Edwardian match striker and holder with 'Scratch my back' printed on the big pig and 'Me too' on the smaller one.*

PRICE GUIDE ❸

▼ *A novelty pig fairing with its front trotters in hollowed-out tray. It dates from the Edwardian period.*

PRICE GUIDE ❷

▼ *An Edwardian spill holder with three crossed hollow branches. The piglet and tiny banjo-playing jester are crudely painted.*

PRICE GUIDE ❸

▲ *Another Edwardian fairing, also a match holder, showing two smiling pigs sitting beside a wooden tub.*

PRICE GUIDE ❸

◀ *The base of a pin-holder fairing, without its lid, modelled in the form of a fireplace.*

PRICE GUIDE ❸

PRICE GUIDE

COLLECTOR'S TIPS

Generally speaking, the earlier a group was made, the better the modelling, though fairings never attained the quality and crispness of detail of figures from the great factories. The Royal Vienna factory, for instance, produced finely-modelled uncaptioned pieces with typically earthy themes that may have influenced the production of fairings.

Conta & Boehme fairings are the most collectable today. Their earlier, better pieces are unmarked, but those made after the late 1870s are marked on the underside of the base with a representation of a crooked arm holding a dagger. Some later ornaments with coloured bases also carry this mark but are not generally considered to be fairings.

Many Conta & Boehme models have numbers, most of them in the series 2850-2899 and 3300-3385. Again, the earliest pieces have no numbers. Those made around 1870 have the numbers scratched into the base, while later pieces have the number impressed.

The value of individual fairings is naturally affected by their rarity, but there are other factors at work. Some were made without captions, and these fetch less than others. Figure groups on a base are worth more than their equivalents on a box lid or than match holders.

Fairings with sporting or transport themes are particularly collectable, especially those featuring the early 'boneshaker' bicycles introduced around 1870. Although fairings did not always come in pairs, there are several companion pieces that show before and after scenes, humorous juxtapositions or male and female versions of the same topic. Value is naturally enhanced if both pieces can be obtained.

BUYING FAIRINGS

Fairings were mass-produced, but because of their commonplace nature they were not looked after as well as finer pieces of

Reproduction Fairings

THE FAIRING ON THE LEFT IS A REPRODUCTION MODEL ENTITLED 'GOOD TEMPLARS'. THAT ON THE RIGHT IS INSCRIBED WITH 'O DO LEAVE ME A DROP' AND WAS MADE BY CONTA & BOEHME OF PÖSSNECK IN SAXONY.

A Visit to the Dentist

WHILST MANY VICTORIAN FAIRINGS WERE CONCERNED WITH THEMES OF LOVE AND MARRIAGE, OTHERS CONCENTRATED ON MORE HUMOROUS EVENTS.

THIS DRAMATIC EXAMPLE SHOWS A MAN HAVING HIS TOOTH PULLED OUT. AS AN ASSISTANT HOLDS THE PATIENT'S HEAD THE DENTIST PULLS HIS TOOTH OUT WITH A STRONG TUG. CAPTIONED 'A LONG PULL AND A STRONG PULL', IT IS A RARE DESIGN; THERE WAS ALSO A COMPANION PIECE CALLED 'OUT! BY JINGO!!!' SHOWING ALL THREE FIGURES ON THE FLOOR WITH PATIENT WITH HIS LEGS IN THS AIR. THIS MODEL IS NUMBERED 3335, WHICH HELPS TO DATE IT AT C. 1880.

① THE CLOTHES STYLE WORN BY THE FIGURES CAN BE USED TO HELP DATE A FAIRING WHEN LITTLE ELSE IS AVAILABLE.

② BRIGHT-COLOURED PAINTS WERE FIRST USED IN THE MID 19TH-CENTURY AND CAN ALSO BE A GUIDE TO DATING.

③ ALTHOUGH FAIRINGS WERE MADE IN GERMANY THE FASHIONS ARE FAITHFULLY BRITISH.

④ THIS COPPERPLATE SCRIPT IS FOUND ON ALMOST ALL FAIRINGS AND IS USUALLY IN BLACK. MOTTOES ARE USUALLY RISQUÉ OR WHIMSICAL.

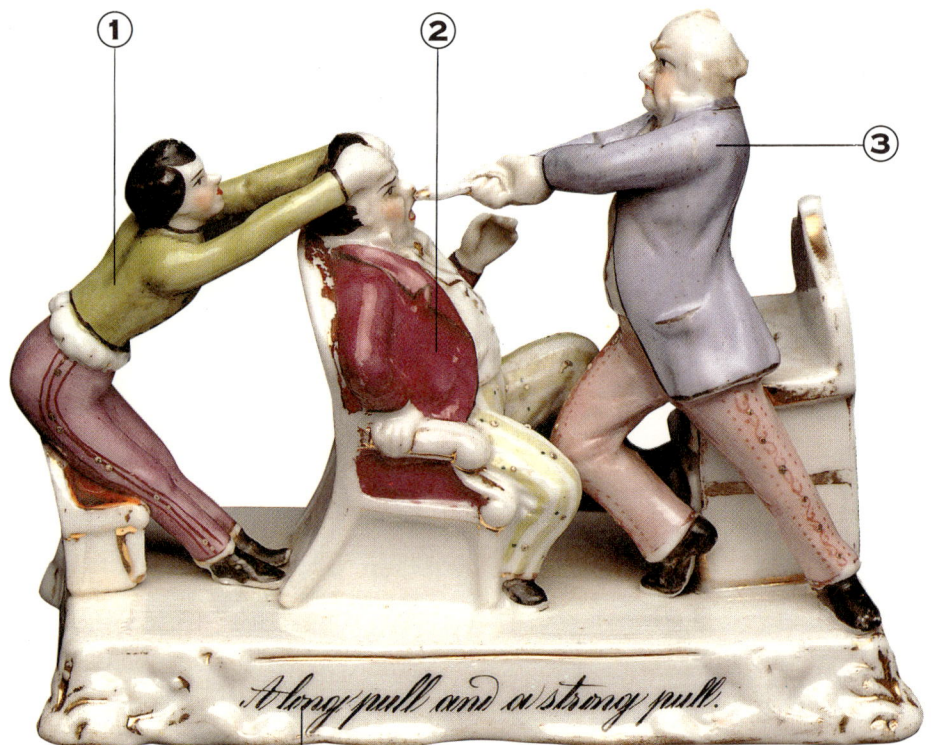

CLOSE UP

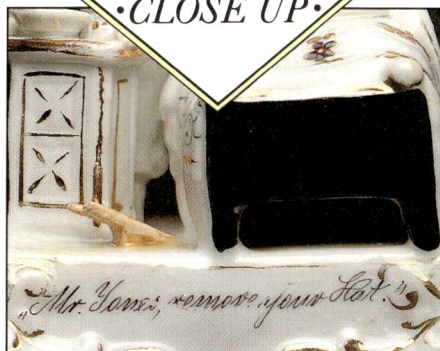

① HAND-WRITTEN CAPTION

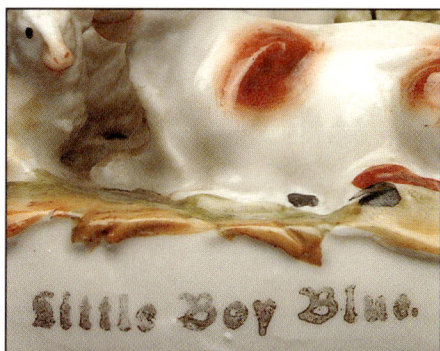

② DELICATE PAINTING

③ RUBBER-STAMPED CAPTION

④ HOLLOW BASE

① THIS RATHER WORN CAPTION (IN COPPERPLATE SCRIPT) WAS HAND-WRITTEN ON THE FAIRING.

② THE STRONGER COLOURS AND DELICATE PAINTING ARE USUALLY ONLY FOUND ON ORIGINAL FAIRINGS.

③ A LATER VERSION OF 'MR JONES, REMOVE YOUR HAT' HAS A RUBBER-STAMPED CAPTION.

④ HOLLOW BASES ARE USUALLY ONLY FOUND ON LATER, INFERIOR FAIRINGS. CONTA & BOEHME MODELS HAD SOLID BASES.

⑤ THE CONTA & BOEHME OF PÖSSNECK MARK SHOWS THE CROOKED ARM AND DAGGER; 'MADE IN GERMANY' WAS USED AFTER 1891.

⑥ SOME OF THE LATER CONTA & BOEHME FAIRINGS WERE NUMBERED. THIS IS FROM A SERIES OF 3300 TO 3384.

⑦ AN INCISED NUMBER, SCRATCHED ON TO THE BODY BEFORE FIRING. PROBABLY FROM THE CONTA & BOEHME FACTORY C.1870.

⑤ CONTA & BOEHME MARK

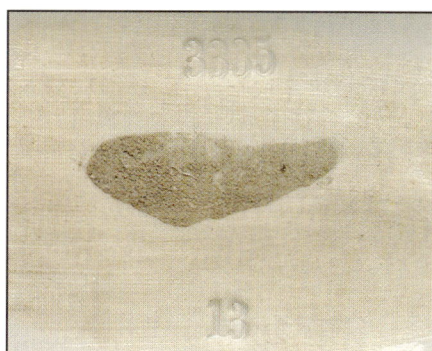

⑥ IMPRESSED NUMBER

⑦ INCISED MARK

porcelain. Many are now rare, and have been heavily reproduced. The best way to tell an authentic piece is to check for signs of wear, especially on the gilding, and for crazing of the glaze.

Genuine Conta & Boehme fairings almost always have the caption in black italic script; in one or two cases it is in red. Other factories produced fairings captioned in a heavy, Germanic script or Roman capitals; these too, were generally black, though one factory used gilt captions.

Not all Conta & Boehme fairings are marked, but any piece with no mark, save for a 'Made in Germany' stamp, comes from one of the other factories.

DATING FAIRINGS

Numbered fairings can be dated with reasonable accuracy, and an expert can date a piece within a year or two according to the fine detail of the bases. A base with a continuous ridge around the top and bottom, for instance, is from the first half of the 1860s.

Another method is to analyse the subject matter of a fairing. Women's fashions are a good clue; any fairing showing women in crinolines is likely to be from the 1860s, while bustles did not come into fashion until around 1870. Similarly, any piece showing a bicycle must date from after 1867, when the boneshakers were introduced.

Some fairings, especially later ones, took their inspiration from other, published sources – song titles, sheet-music covers and popular prints – that can be dated exactly.

POINTS TO WATCH

■ Check condition; small repairs do not necessarily decrease value.
■ Make sure that the style, the number and mark, if any, and the subject all point to the same date and factory.
■ The caption should be legible
■ Check that any crazing is natural. Uniform crazing may indicate a reproduction piece with a modern glaze that crackles during firing.

▲ *Made in the fairing style, this Victorian candle holder is delicately moulded in china and decorated with gilding.*

Art Deco Figurines

The figurines that once adorned the Art Deco dressing table – whether they are demure shepherdesses or exuberant modern flappers – are highly collectable pieces today

However modern and uncluttered a young lady may have liked her bedroom to appear, she rarely denied herself a few china ornaments. Less favoured ones might stand on shelves or on top of a chest of drawers, but an especially cherished piece would take pride of place at her right hand on the dressing table. The figure was almost invariably female and expressed a great deal of the owner's image of herself.

The wide range of styles available catered for every personality. If she had a nostalgic temperament, a lady might choose a classical shepherdess in the style of the 18th century or a demure Victorian girl in a poke bonnet. But if she was a 'bright young thing' determined to enjoy the Jazz Age, there were figurines that brazenly declared that modern women could do things and wear things their mothers would have never countenanced, or even have dreamed of as remote possibilities.

CERAMIC SCULPTURE

China figurines of the 1920s and 1930s do not always display the wild exuberance of Art Deco bronzes, for the simple reason

Modern Figures

ROYAL DOULTON STILL MANUFACTURE A WIDE VARIETY OF FIGURES. THE SPLENDIDLY ELABORATE PRINCESS BADOURA SEATED ON HER ELEPHANT WAS FIRST INTRODUCED IN 1952.

that a lady balanced on one toe, with her other leg stretched out high in the air, is a difficult subject for ceramic sculpture. A broad base is traditionally a prerequisite of a good china figure: wide-skirted Victorian ladies, for example, do not fall over while they are being dusted. Portraying the fashions of the 1920s in pottery or porcelain presented new problems. Ladies with bare legs issuing from a short skirt or negligee usually meant that the sculptor had to incorporate some kind of plinth or seating arrangement in the composition to give it stability. In the Royal Doulton figure, *The Bather,* the necessary stability is cleverly provided by the folds of the dressing gown the lady is in the act of shedding.

EROTIC MODELS

A figure like *The Bather,* which was introduced in 1924, illustrates a new attitude to the nude in the art of the 1920s. In Victorian times, Classical nudes of a rather chaste nature were a familiar sight in many odd corners of the house and garden. Art Nouveau nudes had a more overt eroticism, but the ladies portrayed resembled the heroines of Tennysonian romance rather than real people. *The Bather,* however, stepping out of her colourful dressing gown, could easily have been a suburban house-wife. Some people were clearly shocked by this and the manufacturers answered their complaints by making a version of the figure wearing a black bathing suit.

POTTERY REVIVAL

Not all figurines were frivolous or naughty. During the 1920s English art pottery underwent a great revival through the work of artists such as Gwendolen Parnell, Charles Vyse and Harry Parr, who all set up independent studios in Chelsea. Their pieces were either commissioned or produced in strictly limited editions. Some of Parnell's work was a deliberate attempt to revive the great days of Chelsea pottery in the 18th century. Appropriately, one of her first sets of figures showed characters from *The Beggar's Opera,* which was performed at the Lyric, Hammersmith in 1920. She also modelled the characters of *A School for Scandal.* For a time she enjoyed such success that leading society figures sat to be sculpted by her and immortalised in pottery. Charles Vyse was most successful with his old-fashioned street-sellers, traditional subjects for figurines, which never seem to lose their popularity. In fact *The Cries of London,* personifications of *The Four Seasons,* musicians, figures from well-known plays and from Dickens, *Pierrot* and *Pierrette, Harlequin* and *Columbine,* all old favourites, proved as popular as ever.

All these subjects were available, some in more than one version, in the most extensive range obtainable in Britain in the 1920s and 1930s, the bone china figures produced at Royal Doulton's Burslem works under the artistic direction of Charles Noke. Noke had himself created many of the most popular models in the early years of the range, including the appealing little child in a nightdress known as *Darling.* This and other older figures continued to sell well throughout the 1920s, but the figures which best expressed the spirit of a new age were those of Leslie Harradine.

HARRADINE'S FIGURES

Harradine's figures of women in contemporary dress (and undress) owed little to the artistic fashions of the day; there is nothing stylized, Cubist or primitive about them. The only features that give them an Art Deco flavour are the poses and the fashions they depict. Some are fond and humorous records of the excesses of the flappers, an obvious example being *Miss 1926* with her stylish Eton crop. Business being business, she was resissued as *Miss 1927* and *Miss 1928.* Although figures from the 1920s remained in production up to the War, the models of the 1930s, as befitted the times, were more sober in dress and behaviour. Gone were the pert, scantily-clad young girls, the shingled hair, orange dresses and scarlet shoes.

FOREIGN IMPORTS

People who wanted even more outlandish figures in pottery or porcelain could choose from those imported in small numbers from most of the countries of Europe. Some of these came close in style to the archetypal Art Deco bronzes of energetic dancing nudes, but, given the constraints of mould-making for ceramic figures, nudes were more likely to be seated or kneeling. Some imported figures show the influence of the art of the time. The French clowns and Pierrots have a stylized, chunky appearance, with straight lines and regular curves that were derived from Cubist painting. These pieces often have a fresh and modern feel about them.

Doulton Figures

Because of their wealth of detail, carefully delineated by hand, the Doulton figures of the twenties provide a splendid record of the tastes of a bygone age. The bright frivolity of the period was captured by Leslie Harradine in figures such as *Negligée* with her bandeau and bobbed hair and the pyjama-suited *Lido Lady*, sitting with her legs up in a jaunty pose holding a small dog on her lap. Dogs also feature in the marvellous *Scotties* of 1928. A girl sits on a sarcophagus with classical swags, attended by her two Scotties, which are clearly as essential to the overall look of her outfit as her bright red shoes. The figures Harradine designed in the thirties did not include so many studies of contemporary subjects. One exception was a stunning long, slender

▼ *The aptly-named Delight, who wears the costume of an 18th-century shepherdess, was manufactured from 1936 to 1967. This example was made in the 1930s.*

PRICE GUIDE **5**

▲ *The Butterfly Girl was an enduringly popular design. She first appeared in 1925 and was still being made fifty years later. This version dates from the 1930s.*

PRICE GUIDE **7**

▲ *Miss Demure peeps out coyly from behind her parasol. Although her outfit looks mid-Victorian, the figure was actually in production between 1930 and 1975.*

PRICE GUIDE **5**

PRICE GUIDE

figure called *Celia*, dating from 1935 who was incorporated into the decoration of a clock. Other Doulton figures, both traditional and contemporary, were used to decorate the pedestals of lamps, but it seems that few of these were sold.

Among the other artists used by Doulton, one in particular stands out. This was the celebrated sculptor and Royal Academician Richard Garbe, whose ivory carvings were made into china versions by Doulton in the late thirties. The figures were more Art Nouveau than Art Deco in spirit, and they represented diaphanously draped or naked women with titles like *Spring*, *Dryad of the Pines* and *Spirit of the Wind*. A special matt finish was used to imitate the ivory. In other pieces, brilliance of colour was given by separate firings.

◀ *Phyllis dates from the 1930s, but flower-sellers have been a popular subject for artists since the 18th century.*

PRICE GUIDE **7**

◀ *Lady Clare, first modelled by Leslie Harradine in 1931, shows a Victorian lady, hands clasped in front of her, lost in quiet contemplation.*

PRICE GUIDE **6**

▲ *This is only one of many different versions of the figurine Pierette. Others show her wearing a Harlequin skirt, or with playing cards cascading down her dress.*

PRICE GUIDE **7**

125

Continental Figures

While English china figures of the 1920s and 1930s reflected fashions in clothing rather than artistic trends, many continental manufacturers produced pieces that are unmistakeably Art Deco, both in subject and in style. Parisian shops like Atelier Primavera and Robj, which specialized in chic interior decoration, always stocked the very latest in china ornaments. Robj bibelots were deliberately naive, treating subjects like comical black jazz-musicians and stylized Pierrots and Columbines. The figures were often practical as well as decorative, serving as lamps, bottles, bonbonnières and even cocktail-shakers.

Primavera generally sold the familiar dancing females in various states of undress. These figurines inspired by the bronze and ivory statues of Ferdinand Preiss, were manufactured all over Europe. The two companies which best succeeded in emulating the athleticism of Art Deco bronzes in china were Goldscheider of Vienna and Royal Dux from Duchov in Czechoslovakia. Notwithstanding the particular problems of china manufacture, Goldscheider recreated many famous bronze figurines in porcelain, including the much copied *Bat Dancer* (or *Butterfly Girl*, depending on the shape and colour of her wings.) They also made bathing belles, fashionably-clad ladies and china heads in the style of the fiercely primitive wall-masks that were all the rage for a time. Royal Dux (the trademark name of Duxer Porzellanmanufaktur) produced many dancers, single ladies and couples doing the tango, as well as saucy bathers surprised in the act of changing or drying themselves.

▲ *These two young student lovers have a decidely modern air about them. They were made by the Lenci factory in Turin.*

PRICE GUIDE **8**

▶ *A 1930s Royal Dux figurine showing a graceful, but rather daring, topless lady carrying a tray.*

PRICE GUIDE **6**

▲ *A fascination with the exotic Orient is evident in this colourful dancing figure, which was made by the German firm of Rosenthal in the 1930s.*

PRICE GUIDE **7**

▶ *The simplified geometric forms of modern art are easy to detect in this figurine by French designer Sybille May.*

PRICE GUIDE **6**

PRICE GUIDE

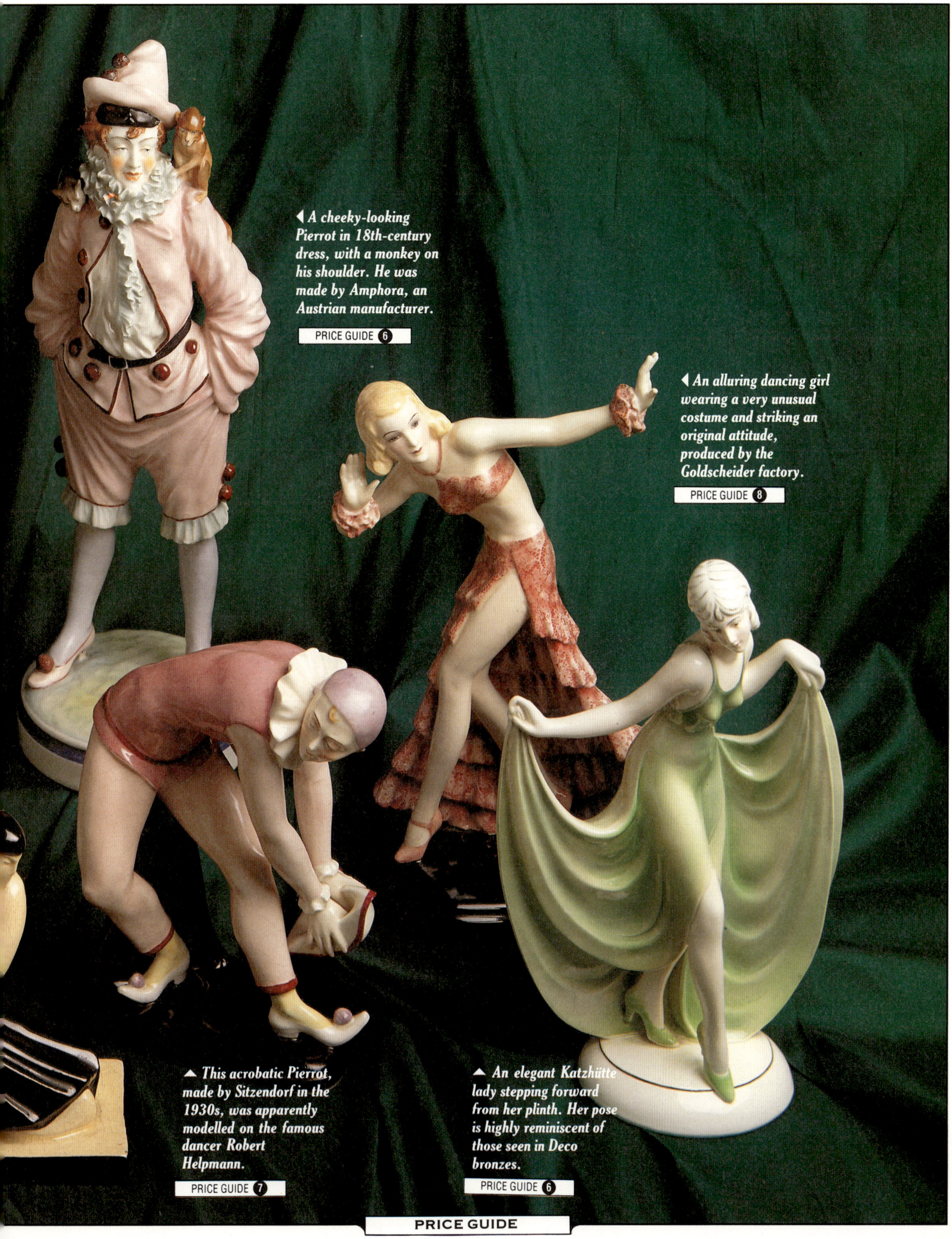

◀ *A cheeky-looking Pierrot in 18th-century dress, with a monkey on his shoulder. He was made by Amphora, an Austrian manufacturer.*

PRICE GUIDE ⑥

◀ *An alluring dancing girl wearing a very unusual costume and striking an original attitude, produced by the Goldscheider factory.*

PRICE GUIDE ⑧

▲ *This acrobatic Pierrot, made by Sitzendorf in the 1930s, was apparently modelled on the famous dancer Robert Helpmann.*

PRICE GUIDE ⑦

▲ *An elegant Katzhütte lady stepping forward from her plinth. Her pose is highly reminiscent of those seen in Deco bronzes.*

PRICE GUIDE ⑥

PRICE GUIDE

COLLECTOR'S TIPS

Flower Sellers

TWO DOULTON LADIES SELLING PRIMROSES AND LAVENDER. THESE NOSTALGIC SUBJECTS WERE VERY POPULAR IN THE 1930S.

The collector of china figures from the 1920s and 1930s must choose between a field where what is available is extremely well-documented, as is the case with Royal Doulton's HN series, and works from lesser-known companies (or defunct ones) where documentation is almost non-existent.

The HN series, still produced today, derives its name from the initials of Harry Nixon, the man in charge of the artists in 1913. It includes the bone china figures produced at Burslem and the stoneware figures made at Lambeth. Almost every figure and every variation in design and decoration was given an HN number when it went into production. Some also exist in two different sizes. Some pieces are very rare, and if you want to build up a complete set, you may have to pay many hundreds of pounds for an example. Nobody knows exactly how many of each figure were made, although records do exist for some individual years. Fewer than a hundred exam-

ples may have been sold for less successful models before they were withdrawn, while it is estimated that there may be no more than two or three thousand examples of the longest-running and most successful models. Given the depredation of time, that does not leave many pieces for collectors to chase.

IDENTIFYING PIECES

As with any piece of china, the most important clues to the identity of a figure are the marks impressed, incised or printed on the base. The most useful is obviously the maker's name or a trademark. The latter can usually be identified without too much trouble from the encyclopaedias of pottery and porcelain marks. Those made by well-known firms like Rosenthal or Royal Copenhagen are, of course, easily identified. Ones from Goldscheider or Royal Dux are marked as a rule, but even the experts have a very patchy idea of the full range of their productions. This is

Marietta

ONE OF LESLIE HARRADINE'S MOST POPULAR DESIGNS, MARIETTA WAS PRODUCED BY ROYAL DOULTON IN THREE DIFFERENT VERSIONS, EACH WITH THEIR OWN HN NUMBER, BETWEEN 1929 AND 1949.

SHE IS ONE OF THE MANY MODELS THAT HARRADINE DESIGNED SHOWING MODERN GIRLS IN THE KIND OF EXOTIC COSTUME A BRIGHT YOUNG THING MIGHT HAVE WORN TO A FANCY DRESS PARTY. NO SYMBOLIC OR ALLEGORICAL CONTENT IS INTENDED — THE PIECE IS SIMPLY A LIGHT-HEARTED ORNAMENT THAT PERFECTLY REFLECTS THE 1930S OBSESSION WITH WIT AND AMUSEMENT.

WHEN SHOPPING FOR DOULTON FIGURES, IT IS ALWAYS WORTH TAKING ALONG A RELIABLE GUIDE THAT GIVES HN NUMBERS AND PRICES, AS VALUES FOR THE SAME FIGURE CAN VARY ACCORDING TO THE VERSION.

① LIKE MANY OF HARRADINE'S PIECES, MARIETTA HAS A RATHER COQUETTISH EXPRESSION.

② THE RICH EFFECT OF THE DRAPERY IS ACHIEVED BY THE APPLICATION OF SEVERAL DIFFERENT COLOURS, EACH FIRED SEPARATELY.

③ DOULTON FIGURES ARE ALL MARKED BY THEIR ELABORATE DETAIL. THE FOLDS IN THE CLOAK ARE AN ESPECIALLY DRAMATIC EXAMPLE.

④ THE FIGURE'S STABILITY IS ENHANCED BY A SOLID PLINTH.

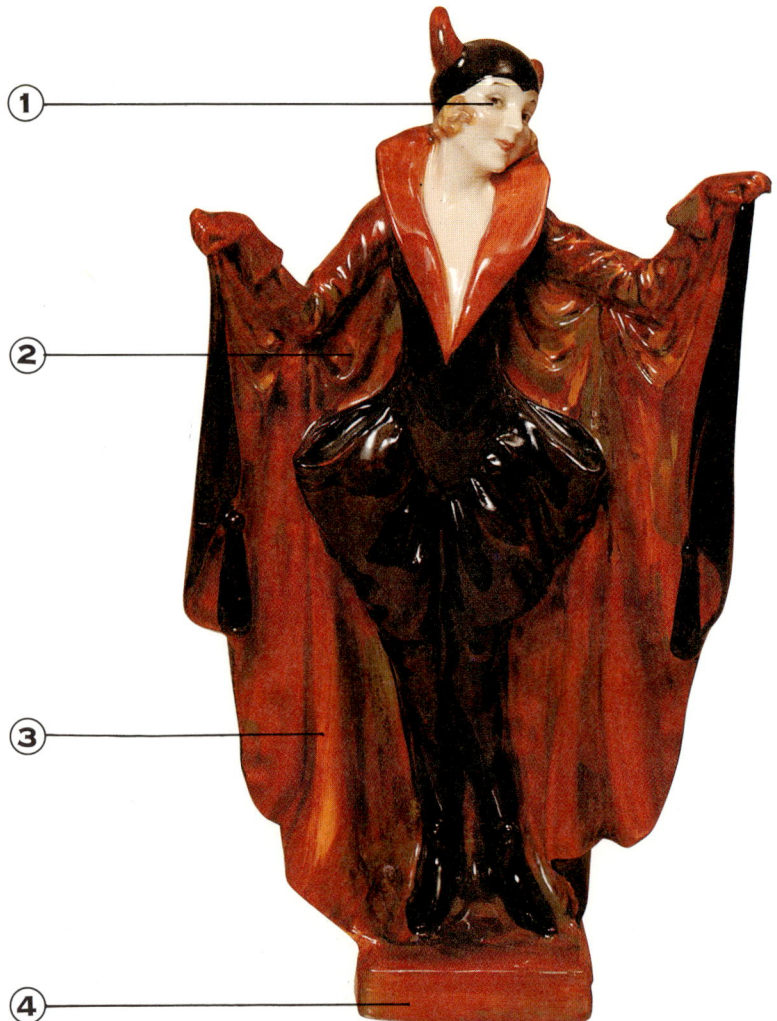

·CLOSE UP·

① IT IS ESSENTIAL TO LOOK AT THE BASE OF ANY FIGURE YOU BUY. THIS ONE BEARS THE MARK OF THE ROYAL DUX FACTORY.

② NOT ALL CONTINENTAL FIGURES ARE PROPERLY IDENTIFIED. THEY MAY SIMPLY CARRY THE NAME OF THEIR COUNTRY OF ORIGIN.

③ THE KATZHÜTTE FACTORY HAS ITS OWN PICTOGRAM — A CAT IN A HOUSE.

④ CERTAIN CONTINENTAL FIGURES HAVE A DECORATIVE CRACKED GLAZE. HERE THIS IS PARTICULARLY NOTICEABLE ON THE GOLDEN BALL.

⑤ FIGURINES OFTEN REFLECT CONTEMPORARY FASHIONS, SUCH AS HEADBANDS, BEADS AND DECORATIVE FACE MASKS.

⑥ SOME MANUFACTURERS MADE SINGLE HEADS, LIKE THIS MODISH EXAMPLE FROM GOLDSCHEIDER.

⑦ THE LEFT ARM OF THIS GOLDSCHEIDER PIECE HAS BEEN BROKEN AND MENDED. THE PURCHASE PRICE SHOULD REFLECT THIS.

① ROYAL DUX MARK

② MADE IN CZECHOSLOVAKIA

③ KATZHÜTTE MARK

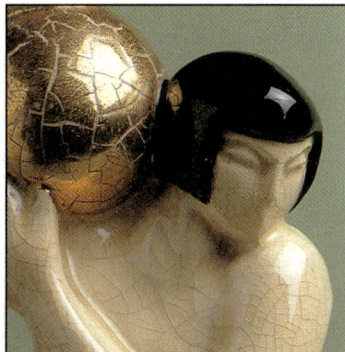

④ CRACKED GLAZE

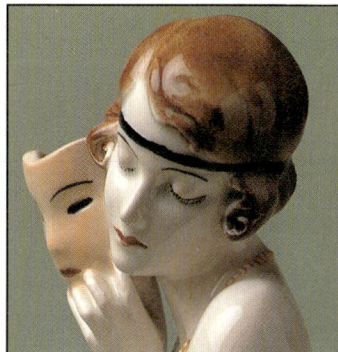

⑤ LADY WITH MASK

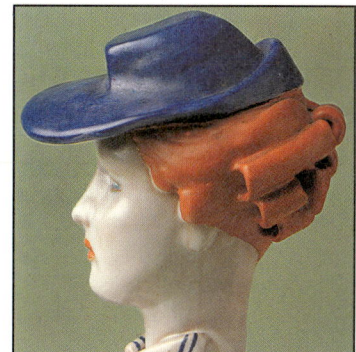

⑥ A SINGLE HEAD

⑦ VISIBLE DAMAGE

hardly surprising given what happened to Austria and Czechoslovakia during the War: the last member of the Goldscheider family packed his bags in 1938 and left for America. However, information is gradually being reassembled as Dux and Goldscheider figures are very popular with collectors looking for ladies in emphatically Art Deco costumes and poses.

Many of the cheaper, imported figures have no maker's mark at all, and other marks may lead to confusion. A number may be the catalogue number of a model or the serial number of an individual piece; a name may be that of a factory, a shop, the sculptor of the model or the artist responsible for the painting. Cheaper figures from France and Belgium which were exported to Britain are notoriously difficult to identify. Typically, they are undecorated figures, white or off-white, with a crackle glaze showing a network of crazing. Figures of this kind, nudes and dancers frequently turn up with nothing more than 'Made in France' printed or impressed on them.

Faced with such a problem even the experts of famous auction houses are often defeated, cautiously cataloguing pieces of this kind as 'probably French'.

RISE IN PRICES

With the revival of interest in the Art Deco period, prices have rocketed in the last fifteen years, so for someone starting out as a collector, it might be as well to concentrate on figures at the lower end of the market, especially ones that cannot be ascribed to any particular artist or factory. The quality of their sculpture may not be of the best, but if they convey the vitality and charm of the period, and, above all, if they appeal to you personally, they are a more reasonable buy than more easily authenticated pieces.

POINTS TO WATCH

■ Many modern ceramic figures are made in a pseudo Art Deco style. Some dealers may try to pass them off as original pieces.

■ Do not worry unduly about a chipped base or even a hand inexpertly glued back

▶ *Some figurines were adapted for practical use, like this charming white and gold kneeling Pierrot made by an unnamed Austrian manufacturer. With a lightbulb inside the body, it makes a perfect night light for a child's bedroom.*

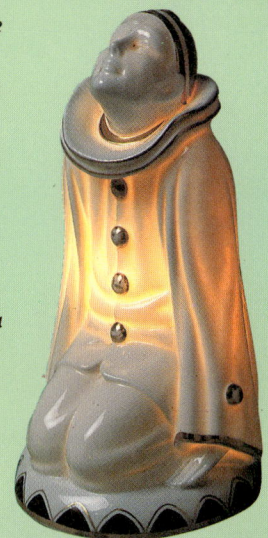

on, but make sure the price takes this into account. An unsightly mend is easily remedied.

■ Beware of the Doulton figures made in the 1950s by Margaret Davies. They are not the Deco originals they resemble.

The Teapot

Tea was a classless, universally popular drink between the wars
and exciting teapots and tea sets were brought out to match the
style of the age

I t is fitting that Art Deco and the hit song 'Tea for Two' both made their debut in 1925. From the start, tea ware and Deco style were destined to enjoy a fruitful marriage. However, although all Deco teapots can be said to have been produced in the 1920s and 1930s, by no means all of the teapots of this period ought to be called Deco. Classic, folksy and humorous lines continued to be brought out, as well as the brave new colours and shapes that defined Art Deco ceramics and silver.

THE POPULAR CUPPA

The years between the wars are recalled as a true golden age of tea-drinking. This was the heyday of Lyons Corner Shops, where an oasis of comfort – red plush seating and chandeliers – was on hand for the price of a cuppa, and where ladies or working girls could meet (or brief encounters be enacted!) in surroundings above reproach. It was also the heyday of the *thé dansant* (or tea dance) where bright young things could tango or quickstep unchaperoned in the richly appointed Palm Courts and tearooms of hotels and department stores.

At home, tea made the rounds upstairs and down – from bedroom tray to kitchen table to drawing room trolley, from nursery to dining room to garden. For the most part, it was tea grown in India and Ceylon – established as breakfast and all-day favourites – with the China varieties mainly making their appearance along with the three-tiered cake stand and hot buttered scones for afternoon tea.

In the 1840s, when the custom of afternoon tea started, Britain had shaken off China's 200-year monopoly on tea by developing plantations in her colonies. Lower prices put tea within reach of the Victorian masses, and made fortunes for companies that remain household names – Twinings, Tetley and the like. The Co-op, emphatically 'Filling the Nation's Teapot', effected quality control against unscrupulous adulteration by owning its own plantations. Interestingly, tea was also the commodity upon which the Tesco empire was founded, earning a knighthood for Jack Cohen who had once been an unemployed ex-RAF mechanic.

Of the many kitchen appliances now becoming standard, the most popular was the electric kettle. The fully immersible heating element was patented in 1922 and the automatic switch-off in 1929. Kettles for kitchens were functional in appearance, whereas those made for use in dining rooms were noticeably more elegant.

TEAPOT STYLE

The teapots these kettles filled were extremely varied in style. At the top end of the market there were services in silver, some more suited to the art gallery than the table. Most day-to-day teaware was, however, ceramic and competition between manufacturers was fierce. The invention of the tunnel-kiln and spray-gun facilitated mass production, but

Puiforcat Silver Tea Set

JEAN PUIFORCAT WAS THE LEADING DESIGNER OF DECO SILVER ON THE CONTINENT. THIS TEA SET, COMPRISING A TEAPOT, HOT WATER JUG, MILK JUG AND SUGAR BOWL, WAS DESIGNED IN THE 1920S AND PRODUCED BY ELKINGTON & CO OF BIRMINGHAM IN 1936.

Teapot Designs

THE MODE SHAPE – AN INVERTED CONE WITH TRIANGULAR HANDLE – WAS INTRODUCED BY SHELLEY. VOGUE AND EVE SHAPES WERE SIMILAR.

CUBE TEAPOTS ARE QUINTESSENTIALLY DECO. WEDGWOOD, COPELAND, MINTON AND OTHERS ALL MADE CERAMIC CUBE TEAPOTS FROM 1925.

THE OLD WOMAN WHO LIVED IN A SHOE IS ONE OF THE BEST KNOWN NOVELTY TEAPOTS. IT WAS MADE IN TUNSTALL, STAFFORDSHIRE.

▲ *Not only was tea at the height of its popularity in Britain during the inter-war years, it also had a certain vogue in Paris. Fashionable Parisiennes enjoy afternoon tea and the latest gossip, above, in 1924.*

◀ *A teapot, hot water jug and sugar bowl from a 1930s tea set. They are in white china with plastic-handled chrome covers.*

customers often preferred the qualities of colour and line which only hand-painting could give.

The king and queen of Art Deco tea-set design were the French sculptor-silversmith Jean Puiforcat in metal and, in ceramics, Staffordshire potter Clarice Cliff. While Puiforcat crafted one-off masterpieces for the affluent, Clarice Cliff created lines for the mainstream, which were made in vast quantities and sold in department stores such as Woolworth's. Her artistic originality and marketing flair made her a celebrity at the time.

Silver tea sets comprised a teapot, sugar bowl and milk jug at least, with perhaps an additional hot water jug or a coffee pot to match. Other accessories included tea strainers, sugar tongs and trays. China tea sets normally extended to cups and saucers, with

China

side plates and a slop bowl frequently part of the range. Special early-morning or breakfast sets and nursery sets were also made – these had smaller teapots.

The key element of Art Deco silver design was shape. Metal, indeed, was best suited to Deco's angularity, which was more awkward to express in clay. Ceramics, on the other hand, could make their statements in colour; a readily recognizable palette of acid-bright oranges, greens, yellows and blues, often strongly outlined in black on a white crackle glaze, came to characterize Deco style.

Jean Puiforcat was principally concerned with re-juvenating silver design, which he felt suffered from outmoded excess ornamentation. He replaced traditional embellishments with clean contours that had a beauty and luxury of their own. He disliked being labelled a Cubist, saying that his one desire was not to be at the mercy of a formula. His tea sets were an inspiration to his peers – Tétard Frères, Theodore Wende, Charles Boyton and others – who, like him, opted for sleek lines simply adorned with handles and finials of ivory, rare hardwoods or crystal; or inlay such as lapis lazuli. Sometimes the trend for audacious Bauhaus design could backfire in

practical terms, resulting in pieces that may have been Cubist chic, but were thoroughly impractical at teatime!

CLIFF'S BIZARRE

Clarice Cliff's contribution to Art Deco ceramics made her name synonymous with the genre. The brilliant colours and geometric shapes of the line she called Bizarre were an instant sensation in 1929. The design was so successful that she hired young 'paintresses' to fulfill demand. The patterns she taught them to trace were painted in enamel on top of a first glaze and then fixed by re-firing. This on-glaze technique gave a more vivid range of colours than could be got by the normal under-glaze used by her competitors.

Her subsequent Fantasque and Biarritz ranges bore her facsimile signature, and so great has been their popularity that both legitimate reproductions and outright forgeries now abound. Under Clarice Cliff's art direction, A.J. Wilkinson Ltd also commissioned designs from leading contemporary painters, including Vanessa Bell, Duncan Grant, Laura Knight and Paul Nash.

Paul Nash also designed for Foley China, the firm which later became the famous Shelley Pottery. Shelley's extremely fine wares incorporated cups in inverted conical shapes with triangular handles, or curved octagonal shapes, decorated with bold-

▲ *Teas was a refreshing pick-me-up out of doors. Elevenses and afternoon tea might be taken in the garden, weekend picnics were popular and no British worker got through the day without a brew-up.*

◀ *A Humpty Dumpty teapot from the 1930s. Nursery rhyme characters were popular subjects for novelty teapots.*

PRICE GUIDE ④

·PRICE GUIDE· ▷ TEAWARE

Teapots and other individual items can form an interesting collection and are considerably cheaper (from £10 upwards) than complete tea sets. Ceramic sets for two can cost £100-£200, while six-place sets are likely to be £200-£400 or more. Sets that are strikingly Deco in design are most sought after.

▼ *Cup, saucer and side plate from a Butterfly Wing patterned Shelley Mode tea set. It is one of the most valuable sets.*

PRICE GUIDE ④

▲ *Teaware in Shelley's Regent shape with a geometric pattern dating from 1933.*

PRICE GUIDE ③

▶ *Typhoo was the only company to produce tea cards in the 1930s. Shown are cards from the Lorna Doone, British History and Zoo sets.*

PRICE GUIDE ① ③

▲ *Shelley produced more than geometric designs. That is part of their Anemone Bunch pattern tea set for two.*

PRICE GUIDE ⑤

132

period. James Sadler & Sons of Burslem had tremendous sales of their racing car teapot in which the driver's head formed the knob for the lid. It, and a similarly styled aeroplane, were made in a range of bright glazes with silver lustre details. Nursery rhyme and music hall characters were other popular subjects. The firm of Lingard produced The Old Woman Who Lived in a Shoe and Beswick immortalized Dickens' Dolly Varden in a striking earthenware design.

The 1920s and 1930s are also recalled for the vogue in cottage ware. Teapots were made in the form of cottages by several companies, the best known being Price Brothers, Grimwades and Wilt-shaw & Robinson as part of their Carlton Ware range.

Alongside these more obviously collectable lines are the humbler artefacts of the age. Sentimental and slightly gimmicky mail order sets were sometimes quite successful. One such was Crown Pottery's Initial China, with letters in flowers and a well in the centre of the saucers 'into which spilled tea runs, leaving the cup high and dry', according to the 1923 catalogue.

By the late 1930s tea sets were returning to more traditional shapes and patterns, with fewer abstract designs. Susie Cooper appealed to a middle-class market more conservative than Clarice Cliff's. The establishment, as embodied by Wedgwood, had never gone in for Deco themes. Throughout the period, such timeless favourites as the blue-and-white willow pattern and windmills were still popular – but the gifted practitioners of Art Deco left a legacy of original design in teaware which has not been seriously rivalled since.

coloured motifs – sunbursts, peacock tails or geometric patterns. A piece could be identified by shape (for example, Mode) and pattern (Butterfly Wing, for instance).

NOVELTY TEAPOTS
Foley and Shelley also produced a number of the novelty pieces which were so much a feature of the

▼ One of James Sadler and Sons' novelty teapots, known as 'Ye Dainty Ladyee' or the Crinoline Lady.
PRICE GUIDE 3

◄ Part of a Paragon tea set. The full six-place set includes two cake plates. Triangular designs date from the early 1930s.
PRICE GUIDE 5

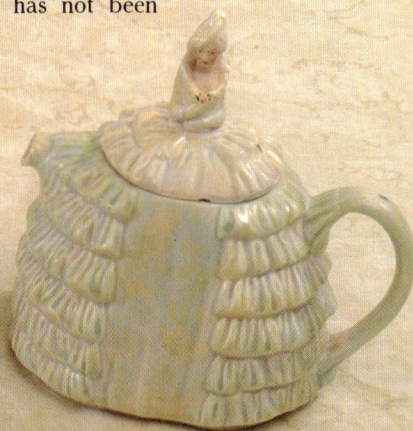

◄ A tea-for-one teapot by Burgess and Leigh. Part of their Burleigh Ware range, the pattern is known as Balmoral.
PRICE GUIDE 1

▲ Part of Royal Doulton's Tango tea set for six. It combines classical touches with a geometric Deco motif.
PRICE GUIDE 6

133

Art Deco Tableware

Originally designed to bring colour and zest into the home after the austerity of the First World War years, Art Deco ceramics continue to be a source of pleasure

The bright colours and energetic designs of commercially produced Art Deco tableware came as a breath of fresh air to the dining room of the 1920s. After the drabness and privation of the war years, nothing could be more welcome than the 'jazzy' jugs and teapots, cups and saucers, plates and sugar basins. Art Deco tableware offered novelty and variety; it was in tune with the times and, above all, it was affordable. It was made in large quantities and could be bought at no great cost, and was also the cheapest and easiest way of keeping up with an exciting new style that was making itself felt in all areas of design. Art Deco tableware is still as bright and stimulating now as it was sixty years ago; it is no longer cheap but is still widely available and thus easy to collect.

GEOMETRICAL INSPIRATION
Art Deco had no single founder. It derived from a variety of influences: Cubism, African art and mechanization being just a few. The style was applied to everything from furniture to textiles and jewellery, often resulting in expensive, exclusive designer pieces. Vibrant and energetic, it was consciously modernistic and avant-garde.

Rare Patterns

THIS LARGE CIRCULAR CHARGER FROM THE BIZARRE COLLECTION IS DECORATED WITH A VERY RARE PATTERN USING UNUSUALLY PALE, SUBDUED COLOURS.

Geometry was its hallmark and this was reflected in both shapes and designs based on ovoids, octagons, ziggurats, angular lines and a striking combination of colours. But most British potteries did not go to the extremes of some continental makers.

Craft potters of the day felt that clay did not lend itself naturally to angular shapes, so many shunned the new, geometric style. However, the ceramics industry widely exploited the Art Deco style and at a price that ordinary people could afford. Being cheap and cheerful, Art Deco tableware tended to be bought by the younger generation; to their elders, used to the gentility of the Edwardian era, it often seemed crude and shocking.

YOUNG INNOVATORS

It was the young Clarice Cliff who, sensing the spirit of the Jazz Age, first saw the possibilities of inexpensively applying Art Deco designs to ordinary, everyday tableware. The result was a wealth of radical new shapes and patterns that were a world away from the staid, traditional dinner services with which tables continued to be laid in conservative households. Working at Wilkinson's Newport Pottery with a team of paintresses, Clarice Cliff produced a range of tableware decorated with patterns based on simple diamond shapes and semicircles painted in bold shades of blue, orange, yellow and black. Despite initial apprehension on the part of retailers, these new wares were eagerly bought by an appreciative clientèle. Encouraged with this success, Clarice Cliff produced range after range of other new patterns; these incorporated stylized flowers, landscapes, houses and windmills in bright colour combinations that became her hallmark. Striking new shapes for teapots, jugs and cups soon followed.

At about the same time, Susie Cooper, working at A.E. Gray & Co., was blazing a similar trail between existing tableware that was either expensive or downright shoddy. Like Clarice Cliff, she devised radical new floral and geometric patterns, later going on to produce a range of elegantly simple tableware.

Both Clarice Cliff and Susie Cooper were aided by improved production methods. Electric kilns allowed firing to be better controlled and mechanical spraying speeded production. Both, however, relied on paintresses to decorate their wares, and both designed patterns with their capabilities in mind.

MASS PRODUCTION

Thanks to the early popularity of Clarice Cliff and Susie Cooper designs, the factories of Wilkinson's and Gray's were soon producing their tableware in enormous quantities. Stimulated by their success, other factories followed the trend, so that by the mid-1930s, department stores for instance Harrods, Heal's and Selfridges were stocking Art Deco services produced by firms such as Wedgwood, Worcester

◀ The works of Clarice Cliff and Susie Cooper are now synonymous with Art Deco. Along with other Deco items of Deco tableware, their designs make an impressive collection today.

▲ It is estimated that Clarice Cliff devised around two thousand different designs. Many collectors limit their display to one or two patterns.

Royal Porcelain and Royal Doulton. Each factory competed against the other to tempt the tastes of its customers, to which novelty was all-important.

Royal Doulton's Art Deco range included 'Wynn', 'Casino', 'Merryweather' and 'Tango', the latter consisting of clean, ovoid shapes decorated with striated semicircles. Among the Shelley pottery's most dramatic services was 'Mode', distinguished by sharp triangular handles, and decorated with floral, geometric or banded patterns. Another distinctly geometric Shelley shape was 'Vogue', with square plates. While most other potteries were using earthenware for their fashionable ranges, these services were produced in bone china and were not meant as simply everyday pieces.

Other factories that successfully followed the Art Deco trend included Wiltshaw & Robinson, with their richly decorated 'Carlton' ware, and Fielding, with their 'Crown Devon' range. The Art Deco style was also used in the products of Burgess & Leigh, and A.G. Richardson's 'Crown Ducal' range, and likewise patterns such as 'Claremont' and 'Hazeldene' devised by William Moorcroft. Both Burgess & Leigh and Richardson's counted among their designers Charlotte Rhead, whose tube-lined ceramics were extremely successful. (Tube-lining is a form of decoration which looks as though it has been applied with an icing bag).

Into the late 1930s, the Art Deco movement showed no signs of losing its momentum. But even if the outbreak of war in 1939, when all pottery manufacturers were faced with shortages and the outrageous colour schemes became less fashionable, finally brought it to a close, modern-style tableware was here to stay.

Clarice Cliff

Clarice Cliff joined A.J. Wilkinson's Royal Staffordshire Pottery in 1916. Here she gained a grounding in the design, decorating and firing of pottery, and her obvious talent was rewarded when she acquired her own studio at the company's neighbouring Newport Pottery in 1927. Within a year of the test launch of her early designs, the Newport Pottery was turned over entirely to the production of her 'Bizarre' range.

Clarice Cliff's early designs consisted of geometric patterns outlined in black and painted in bright colours. Later, she produced many floral patterns which enjoyed long popularity, particularly 'Crocus', in several colourways, and 'Lupin'.

Among Clarice Cliff's most distinctive and unconventional shapes were 'Conical', 'Stamford', with D shapes and flat sides, and 'Bonjour', with circular flat sides. These shapes were often decorated with the popular 'Crocus' pattern.

Later patterns included 'Rhodanthe', dominated by browns and oranges, and its variants, 'Viscaria' and 'Aurea'. These were most often found on Clarice Cliff's later 'Biarritz' range, with its square or rectangular plates. Popular landscape patterns included 'Red Roofs', 'Orange Roof Cottage' and 'House and Bridge'. Other decorative devices included rough or textured surfaces.

Clarice Cliff constantly experimented with slips, glazes and firing techniques. New designs seemed to flow from her, so that by the end of her career she had produced around 2000 patterns and 500 new shapes.

▲ *This striking dinner plate was produced in 1930 and is part of the 'Fantasque' range.*

PRICE GUIDE ❻

▲ *This cigarette and match holder is part of the 'Bizarre' range and was made in 1933.*

PRICE GUIDE ❺

▲ *A biscuit plate with the 'Melon' pattern was made in 1930 as part of the 'Fantasque' range.*

PRICE GUIDE ❻

◀ *A ceramic spill vase from 1929 decorated with the 'Umbrellas and Rain' design.*

PRICE GUIDE **5**

◀ *This conical shaped sugar shaker dates from 1930 and is decorated with the popular 'Crocus' pattern.*

PRICE GUIDE **5**

▲ *A very rare novelty teapot titled 'Bones and Butcher' this comes from the 'Bizarre' range.*

PRICE GUIDE **6**

▲ *Produced in 1935, this sugar bowl with lid has a bold geometric design in the 'Bonjour' shape.*

PRICE GUIDE **5**

▲ *Decorated with the best-selling 'Crocus' pattern, this toastrack was made in 1936.*

PRICE GUIDE **4**

▲ *This 'Bonjour' shaped teapot is part of a small tea service comprising 2 cups, milk and sugar bowl.*

PRICE GUIDE **5**

▶ *This cup is part of a tea set produced in 1927 and matches the teapot on the right.*

PRICE GUIDE **5**

Susie Cooper

Susie Cooper went to work for the Burslem pottery-decorating firm of A.E. Gray in 1922. Her daring use of bright colours and fresh geometric and banded patterns quickly brought her recognition and soon earned her the inclusion of her name along with the Gray's mark on her own designs.

By 1930 she had set up her own business, buying in 'white ware' and decorating it as she had done at Gray's. The following year she began to design as well as decorate her own pieces, contracting Wood & Sons' Crown Works, also in Burslem, to produce them.

Among her most successful shapes were 'Kestrel' and 'Curlew'; elegant and simple, they were as modern in concept as the patterns that Susie Cooper continued to design for them. Most of her patterns consisted of stylized flowers, calligraphic and spiral motifs, simple banding and *sgraffito*, in which the design was cut into the coloured glaze.

Later on in the 1930s Susie Cooper began to use lithographic transfers to decorate her pieces. She adapted both her patterns and her shapes for this process, as well as creating new ones. New shapes such as 'Falcon', 'Rex' and 'Spiral' were decorated with lithographic transfers of patterns such as 'Gilley Flower', 'Nosegay' and 'Acorn'. Most lithographic decoration was set off with hand-painted washbands.

▲ *A large serving platter dating from the 1930s, decorated with a simple ship design.*

PRICE GUIDE 5

▲ *This hors d'oeuvres dish is finely decorated with subtle leaf patterns in green and beige.*

PRICE GUIDE 4

▲ *A small teapot with a lithographed tulip design using fashionable shades of pink and green.*

PRICE GUIDE 4

PRICE GUIDE

▲ The 'Kestrel' shape, designed in the 1930s, was popular for decades. This teapot dates from the 1950s.

PRICE GUIDE ❸

▶ A particularly light and delicate design in muted colours.

PRICE GUIDE ❷

▲ A hand-painted flower vase with an unusual abstract design based on leaves.

PRICE GUIDE ❺

▲ Produced in fine pottery at the Crown works, this coffee set has a matching dinner service.

PRICE GUIDE ❻

▲ A vegetable dish from the 'Kestrel' range. The subtle banded pattern was hand-painted.

PRICE GUIDE ❹

PRICE GUIDE

Most British Art Deco tableware was made cheaply for a mass market. Today, it has become highly collectable and, ironically, far too valuable for daily use.

Not surprisingly, the most expensive pieces are those hand-painted to designs by Clarice Cliff, the most famous of the Pottery Ladies. Among the most commonplace and therefore the least expensive of the wares that she designed are tea and dinner services with patterns such as 'Crocus' and 'Rhodanthe'. Rarest are patterns that were unsuccessfully launched and quickly withdrawn; 'Delicia' is one of these, a pattern produced by allowing the colours to run and mingle, producing a luscious effect, as seen on the metallic speckled 'Goldstone' and the rough-textured 'Patina'.

Virtually all ceramics by Clarice Cliff are stamped, most often in black or, more rarely, in gold. Most marks consist of the words 'Bizarre' and Clarice Cliff's facsimile signature, together with the name of the pattern and that of the manufacturer, either Wilkinson or Newport Pottery.

Complete sets of Clarice Cliff tableware are usually expensive. A cheaper alternative to acquiring a tea or dinner service is to build up a set by buying odd pieces of the same design. Since her most popular tablewares were made in large quantities, this is a feasible approach for most people.

However, Clarice Cliff's are far from being the only examples of Art Deco tableware that is worth collecting. Her fame tends to overshadow the talents of lesser-known designers of the time. Among these is Susie Cooper, who was influenced by Clarice Cliff but who produced a generally more refined and sophisticated range of shapes and patterns. Her tablewares are usually cheaper than Clarice Cliff's and, as the products of a known designer, are perhaps better buys.

The pieces that she decorated at Gray's are marked 'Designed by Susie Cooper'. The earliest products of the Susie Cooper Pottery are stamped with the words 'A Susie Cooper Production', sometimes with 'Burslem, England' as well. Pieces designed by Susie Cooper specifically for Wood & Son are marked with Wood's backstamp incorporating Susie Cooper's name. These three marks identify her wares with the different stages of her career before 1939.

Good buys can also be made in the range

Reproductions

THE JAM POT ON THE RIGHT IS A RARE EXAMPLE OF THE 'TARGET' PATTERN, WHILE THE JUG ON THE LEFT IS A CRUDER REPRODUCTION.

A Conical Bowl

A PARTICULARLY STRIKING EXAMPLE OF CLARICE CLIFF'S WORK, THIS BOWL DISPLAYS CHARACTERISTIC BOLD PATTERNS AND COLOURS, INCLUDING THE BRIGHTEST GREENS, YELLOWS AND ORANGES. THE 'CONICAL' SHAPE WAS THE FIRST OF THE INNOVATIVE SHAPES TO BE PATENTED IN 1931, AND SOLD WELL.

ALTHOUGH NOVELTY AND VARIETY WERE THE MAIN FACTORS INVOLVED IN THE SUCCESS OF CLARICE CLIFF'S STYLE, EACH DESIGN HAD TO BE CAREFULLY MODIFIED TO FIT THE WIDE RANGE OF SHAPES.

① THE COLOURS AND PATTERNS USED INCORPORATE FEATURES OF MANY CONTEMPORARY ARTISTIC MOVEMENTS SUCH AS CUBISM AND MODERNISM.

② CLEAR, BOLD STROKES ARE SYNONYMOUS WITH CLARICE CLIFF'S DESIGNS, A FEATURE THAT IS OFTEN LACKING IN FAKES AND REPRODUCTIONS.

▲ A CERAMIC BOWL IN THE 'CONICAL' SHAPE AND 'UMBRELLA AND RAIN' PATTERN.

·CLOSE UP·

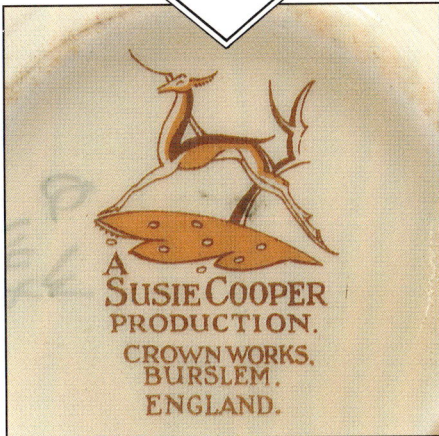
① CROWN WORKS

① SUSIE COOPER LEFT A. E. GRAY & CO. IN 1930 TO SET UP HER OWN POTTERY IN BURSLEM, STAFFORDSHIRE.

② CLARICE CLIFF'S FAMOUS FACSIMILE SIGNATURE, FEATURED ON MOST PIECES.

③ FINE HAND PAINTING, THE UNMISTAKABLE MARK OF AN ORIGINAL WORK.

④ THE PRINTED SIGNATURE OF SUSIE COOPER.

⑤ THE FANTASQUE STAMP WAS USED FROM 1929 TO 1934.

⑥ AFTER THE SUCCESS OF SUSIE COOPER AND CLARICE CLIFF, MANY POTTERIES INCLUDING SHELLEY WERE ENCOURAGED TO PRODUCE BOLDLY DESIGNED POTTERY.

④ SUSIE COOPER

② BIZARRE

③ HAND PAINTING

⑤ FANTASQUE

⑥ SHELLEY POTTERIES

of tea and dinner services that were produced by factories after Clarice Cliff and Susie Cooper had popularized the Art Deco style. Such sets tend to be less distinctive and individual than those of Clarice Cliff and Susie Cooper but are no less authentic examples of 1930s avant-garde tableware. A 21-piece tea set by the Shelley Pottery, for example, can be bought for a fraction of the price of a single jug or plate by Clarice Cliff. Services by other factories, such as Wedgwood and Royal Doulton, are also worthwhile buys.

▶ *A selection from a 42-piece set which includes breakfast ware, a coffee and tea service and a cake stand. This collection is hand-painted in the Alpine design and was originally produced in both the 'Bizarre' and 'Fantasque' ranges.*

FAKES AND REPRODUCTIONS

Generally, Art Deco tableware does not command the kind of prices that make it worth faking. The great exception, of course, is Clarice Cliff, whose more expensive pieces have been faked. Although the backstamp is convincing, these fakes can usually be identified by a poor standard of painting, an uneven glaze and an unglazed bottom rim that is narrower than on genuine pieces. Reproductions pose no problem since they are always marked as such but, of course, they will be of little value.

CONDITION

However rare a shape or pattern, condition, whether in a single piece or a complete service, should be virtually perfect. While some scratching to the glaze through previous use is to be expected, chipping or cracking detracts dramatically from the value of ceramics. Colours should be clean and bright, although allowance must be made for fading through use. Dark blue colouring in pieces by Clarice Cliff is particularly prone to fading.

POINTS TO WATCH

■ Colours should be clean and bright, with an even glaze.

■ Hand-painted decoration will not be identical on separate pieces. Lithographic decoration should be near-perfect.

■ The decoration should be compatible with the shape and size of the piece.

■ Every piece should have a known factory mark.

■ Some shapes and patterns were made over a long period of time.

INDEX

INDEX

INDEX

PICTURE CREDITS

Chris Barker: 59(tl,c). Belinda: 56/7. Bridgeman Art Library: 8, 25(b), 27(tr), 28(l) City Museum and Art Gallery, 35(tl,tc), 36, 37(t), 52/3, 54(b), 56, 59(r), 62(t,b), 80 Victoria & Albert Museum, London, 81(b) Hanley Museum & Art Gallery, 86 Victoria & Albert Museum, London, 99(b), 107, 114, 115, 130(bl), 130/1 Christopher Dennison. Christies Colour Library: 44, 73, 88, 89(t), 122, 134, 141(b). Aubrey Dewer: 30/1, 32/3, 34(t), 52, 54(tc), 61(t,c,b), 62(inset) 65(b), 66/7, 68/9, 70(t,b), 71(b). Ray Duns: 20/1, 22/3, 26(b), 27(b), 53, 54(tl,tr), 55, 71(t), 113(b). E.T. Archive: 58, 60(r,b), 130(br), 131, 132/3, 140, 141(t). Mary Evans Picture Library: 26(t), 27(tl). Fine Art Photographic: 24, 45. John Hollingshead: 80/1, 82/3, 84/5, 86(t), 87. Hulton Deutsch Collection: 25(t). Tom Leighton: 64/5. Ranald Mackechnie: 106/7, 108/9, 110/1, 112/3, 113(t), 134/5, 136/7, 138/9. David Messum Gallery: 132/3(t). Michael Michaels: 72, 72/3, 74/5, 76/7, 78/9. Ian O'leary: 28(r), 60(l). Philips Fine Art Auctioneers: 57(tl). Spike Powell: 17. Peter Reilly: 16, 57(tr), 63, 65(t), 106. Pam Rigby: 59(bl). Duncan Smith: 44/5, 46/7, 48/9, 50(t,b), 51, 98/9, 100/1, 102/3, 104/5, 114/5, 116/7, 118/9, 120/1. Josiah Wedgwood & Sons Ltd: 81(t), 98. Rosemary Weller: 8/9, 10/1, 12/3, 14/5, 16/7, 18/9, 29, 30/1(t), 34(b), 36/7, 38/9, 40/1, 42/3, 88/9, 90/1, 92/3, 94/5, 122/3, 124/5, 126/7, 128/9. Elizabeth Whiting & Associates: 9, 99(t), 135.

Some of this material has previously appeared in the partwork Times Past.